★★★★★ J A Y S ★★★★★

PARANORMAL ALMANAC

COMPLETE FACTS & DATA

EVERY MAJOR PARANORMAL CASE IN HISTORY

Contents

Ghosts of Ancient Egypt

Date	BC
Location	Egypt
Type	Curse, Haunting
Quantity	Multiple
Evidence	Reports
Description	**The Valley of the Kings** The Valley of the Kings sits on the west bank of the River Nile and is one of the most haunted places in Egypt with its ghost tombs and rich ancient history. Consisting of 63 known tombs in Luxor where Pharaohs were buried thousands of years ago and with the lore that they would curse their tombs to prevent anyone from stealing their riches, it's no wonder the Valley of the Kings tombs are haunted. The mummification process is already a good foundation for ghost stories, but when you couple that with the reports of unexplained paranormal phenomena over the years, it's easy to see why this is considered one of the most haunted places in the world. Archaeologists and visitors alike have seen

unexplained shadows and ghosts of Egyptian Pharaohs, wandering near their tombs in full attire.

Ghosts of Egypt

People claim that upon the stroke of midnight, you can see the ghost of a pharaoh riding a fiery chariot pulled by two black horses through the haunted Valley of the Kings wearing his full royal attire and golden headdress. No one know for sure who he is, but most claim he was an ancient Pharaoh that was buried in the Valley.

There are many different types of tombs in ancient Egypt, but the paranormal stories seen to be mainly attributed to a specific few.

King Tut's Haunted Tomb

The haunted Valley of the Kings tombs all contribute to the ghost stories, but one tomb stands out much more than any other, King Tut's tomb.

One of the greatest discoveries to be made was the tomb of King Tut and this tomb could be the main cause of the land's curse. Just a few days after the tomb was located and archaeologists surveyed the site, the dreaded 'curse of the Pharaohs' was unleashed.

The archaeologist who made the discovery saw his pet bird killed by a snake, a creature that is

	symbolic to the ancient Pharaohs. He himself died within a few months of opening it, followed by all of Cairo's lights going out. These events led many to belief that King Tut's tomb was cursed and inspired many of the ghost stories today.
Notes	---

Dudley Castle

Date	1st Century / 2nd Century
Location	West Midlands, England
Type	Haunting, Poltergeists
Quantity	Multiple
Evidence	Reports, Photos, Eye-Witnesses
Description	Dudley Castle in the West Midlands of England is a haunted Castle that barely stands in ruins, but has a rich history dating back as far as the year 700. The Castle was claimed by the antiquarian William Camden to have been built in the year 700 by a Mercian duke named Dodo or Doddo. This claim was also made by other sources throughout history, but today's historians disagree and suggest it was built after the Norman Conquest of 1066 by one of the Conqueror's followers, Ansculf de Picquigny. Dudley Castle has earned its reputation for paranormal activity and hauntings over the years. There's been many ghosts, but one of the most mentioned is that of the Grey Lady who allegedly haunts the grounds. Not to be confused with the Grey Lady of Glamis Castle in Stocland which is even more haunted than

Dudley Castle.

The Grey Lady of Dudley Castle is said to be the spirit of Dorothy Beaumont who died in the castle with her baby, shortly after childbirth. The Grey Lady has haunted the grounds for centuries according to reports of people seeing her.

The Grey lady is the most common sighting of apparitions at Dudley Castle, but there are many more haunted reports including the sound of drums playing which is said to come from the spirit of a young boy who was a drummer, but lost his life to a single bullet during the civil war.

Many people have witnessed sighting of the Grey Lady on Dudley's haunted grounds, some have even managed to capture pictures of her:

Among other ghosts, Dudley Castle has earned much merit as one of the most haunted places in England. Staff and visitors have reported the

| | sound of a cat meowing from where it's believed that a local witch and her cat were thrown to their deaths on the ground below.

There have also been many reports of an extreme drops in temperature, known in the paranormal community as "cold spots".

Other reports are claims of a menacing male spirit, as well as poltergeists. |
|---|---|
| Notes | --- |

Easter Island

Date	800-1200AD
Location	Easter Island, Chile
Type	Paranormal Activity, Unexplained Mystery
Quantity	Multiple
Evidence	Reports
Description	Easter Island, also known Rapa Nui, is an island famous for its enigmatic monuments in Chile, some 2,200 miles off the southeastern Pacific Ocean, and among the world's most remote inhabited islands. Unlike the Island of Dolls which is known for its creepy story of hanged dolls, Easter Island is widely known for its nearly 1,000 monumental statues, called Moai, created by the early Rapa Nui people. It is not clear when the Rapa Nui people settled on the island, but estimates suggests that they moved in between 800 and 1200 AD, while creating a thriving and industrious culture, as evidenced by the island's artifacts. Legend says that the people left for Easter Island because their own island was slowly being swallowed by the sea.

Archaeological evidence showed that the Easter Island was blessed with trees of various sorts, including the largest palm tree species in the world, which furnished the residents with cloth, rope, and canoes.

As the population grew, so did pressures on the island's environment. Deforestation of the island's trees gradually increased, and as this main resource was depleted, the islanders found it hard to continue making rope, canoes, and all the necessities to hunt and fish, and ultimately, support the culture that produced the giant stone figurines.

The late period of the island's civilization was characterized by civil wars and general destruction; more statues were demolished, and many mataa, or obsidian spearpoints were found dating to that period.

Island tradition claims that in around 1680, after peacefully coexisting for many years, one of the island's two main groups, known as the Short-Ears, rebelled against the Long-Ears, burning many of them to death on a pyre that was constructed along an ancient ditch at Poike, on the island's far northeastern coast.

This is where much of the paranormal stories come from and people say that the island is very haunted.

	In 1995, UNESCO named Easter Island a World Heritage site. It is now home to a mixed population, mostly of Polynesian ancestry and made up of the descendants of the Long-Ears and Short-Ears. Till date, the sculptures and the origin of the Polynesians who discovered the island are still an unexplained mystery. No archaeologist has known who the craftsmen were, why they made the artifacts and how they transported those massive stone figurines.
Notes	Though the monuments are just an unexplained piece of history, many believe the island to be haunted because of them.

Chillingham Castle

Date	12th Century
Location	Northumberland, England
Type	Hauntings, Ghosts
Quantity	Multiple
Evidence	Reports, Eye-Witnesses
Description	Chillingham Castle is located in Northumberland, England, just near the Scottish border and is considered the most haunted castle in England. The construction of the castle started in the 12th century and it boasts a rich royal and medieval history. In 1980, it became the home of Sir Edward Humphrey Tyrrell Wakefield. Prior to that is belonged to the Grey and Bennett families, since the 15th century. One of the castle's more recent claims-to-fame is the high levels of paranormal activity and unexplained phenomena that occurs there. **Ghosts of Chillingham Castle** Among the ghosts of Chillingham Castle is the white pantry ghost, a white apparition that appears in the inner pantry of the castle. This ghost is allegedly longing for water which has led many to theorize that they were poisoned to

death.

Another are the ghosts in the courtyard. Shadows come to life at night and visitors have reported seeing many unexplained sightings of apparitions and spirits.

In the Chapel next to the Great Hall, the voices of two men have been heard on numerous occasions. Though it's clear two men are talking, there is no way to trace the voices, because each time someone attempt to, the voices stop.

There are many more ghostly sightings and reports that have earned Chillingham the title of the most haunted castle in England. Ghost tours are available for anyone that wants to experience the paranormal phenomena first hand. You can apply or a ghost tour here: https://chillingham-castle.com/ghosts/

Notes	---

Bran Castle

Date	13th Century
Location	Transylvania, Romania
Type	Haunting, Ghosts
Quantity	Multiple
Evidence	Reports, Eye-Witness
Description	Situated in Transylvania, Romania, Bran Castle is a stunning piece of gothic Architecture that's considered the home of Dracula, an iconic character created by the late Bram Stoker. The castle is a national monument in Romania and now acts as a museum. Bran castle is the only castle located in Transylvania that fits the description of Dracula's castle in the novel and is known throughout the world as such. Stoker never visited Romania and based his imagination and writings of the characters castle simply off description, though many historians say he had no knowledge about the castle at all, though his description of Dracula's castle is strikingly similar to Bran Castle, but doesn't resembled many similarities to any other castle in Romania. Many say the inspiration for the character came from Vlad III Dracul or Vlad the Impaler. And despite popular belief, Vlad has no link to Bram Stoker's character apart from sharing the same

	name and a taste for blood. There is also no evidence of Vlad having any connection to Bran Castle whatsoever, nor is there any proof he ever stepped foot in the castle. Bran Castle has been traced back to initially being built to protect German colonists in Transylvania, but has been in the possession of members of nobility over the years. Bran Castle now belongs to Dominic Habsburg who spent his childhood there and dislikes when people refer to his property as "Dracula's Castle". Bran castle is now a beautiful tourist attraction that sits on a grass hill, surrounded by a large spiked metal fence to protect the grounds. Tours to this historic treasure are available with over 600,000 visitors per year and overnight stays are even allowed for Halloween. The castle has a rich history and Bram Stoker's stories of the undead coming to life at night to feed on the living may actually transpire into reality. There are a few official reports of paranormal activity and sightings in the castle leading to the castle having links to ghosts. Many strongly argue the grounds are haunted.
Notes	Vlad the Impaler killed many people by a way of impaling them on spikes in the 15th century. This is said to be the inspiration for Dracula.

He was Romanian and was nicknamed Vlad
Dracul (Dracula in English), but he and Dracula
have no proven link to Bran Castle other than the
description of a castle in Stoker's 1897 novel.

Glamis Castle

Date	14th Century
Location	Scotland
Type	Curse, Haunting, Ghosts
Quantity	Multiple
Evidence	Reports, Stories, Eye-Witness
Description	Glamis Castle in Scotland has an extremely rich history of ghost sightings and paranormal activity and is home to the Grey Lady, the ghost of Earl Beardie and many more.

Glamis Castle was built in the 14th century and was the childhood home of Queen Elizabeth, the Queen mother. It's a category A protected building, but it's reputation as a paranormal hotspot now exceeds its status as a building of national importance.

Even before construction was attempted on Hunter's Hill there was a supernatural presence. When builders came in to work on the construction of Glamis Castle each morning, they noticed the stones were broken and scattered. They'd rebuilt the walls, but each day it continued to happen.

Eventually a unexplained voice spoke out and

warned them, "build not on this enchanted spot, where man hath neither part nor lot, but build down in yonder bog, where it will neither shake nor shog!"

Ultimately, the warning was heeded and Glamis Castle was built on the flat terrain down the hill. After the castle was built, there were many events that led to making it one of the most haunted places in the world.

The Ghost of Earl Beardie and the Devil's Card Game

Known as Earl Beardie, his true identity is a bit of a mystery. He has been referred to as Alexander Lyon, 2nd Lord of Glamis as well as Alexander Lindsay, 4th Earl of Crawford. Though based on research the latter is probably correct.

Beardie was said to be a cruel man with a serious drinking and gambling problem, which paired well with his rude attitude.

He was playing cards one Saturday night with his friends at Glamis Castle. There was lots of shouting and swearing coming from the chamber room and was heard throughout the castle grounds.

One of the servants came into the room and suggested they should stop gambling before midnight to not play into the Sabbath. The servant was met with Beardie shouting at them.

This is where the story slightly differs slightly.

In one version, Beardie's friends left, but he wanted to play cards past midnight with no regard for the Sabbath and upon returning to his room he shouted "I would even play the devil himself" or something to that affect, in a drunken rage.

Another version states that the servant returned five minutes before the stroke of midnight and warned that Sabbath would start in five minutes, but the servant was met with another abusive roar from Beardie saying he would "play until doomsday" if he wished.

Whichever version is true, it's said that the castle bell rang to announce the stroke of midnight. Afterwards, there came a knock at the chamber door. It was a tall stranger, dressed all in black, who wanted to join the card game in the chamber room.

Whoever was present played until the early hours with the mysterious stranger. There was more shouting and swearing coming from the room, but being scared, and since Beardie had already betrayed the Sabbath already, the servant didn't interrupt again. Though, another version claims the servant looked through the keyhole and was blinded by a bright flash of light.

Following the dawn of the morning, the servant

returned to see if Earl Beardie required anything, but when they opened the door, they saw Beardie still sat at the card table, engulfed in a ball of flame. The mysterious man was still there, but he was not burning to death. He was sneering in amusement. Suggestively, he was actually the devil.

Some say Beardie gambled his soul away in the card game while others suggests his wish was granted and he would play cards until doomsday.

Earl Beardie's ghost is said to be one of the most present at Glamis Castle and it is still believed that there is a secret chamber somewhere on the ground where Beardie's soul is playing cards with the devil.

Over the years, there were reports of children waking up in the middle of the night and seeing a shadowed figure standing over their beds. This is thought to be the ghost of Earl Beardie.

The Ghost of the Grey Lady

The Grey Lady of Glamis Castle is one of the most infamous and commonly seen on the historic grounds. She is also referred to as Lady Glamis.

While the Grey Lady is thought to be the spirit of Lady Janet Douglas, she should not be confused with another spirit of the same name, the Grey

Lady of Dudley Castle in the West Midlands, who is said to be the spirit of Dorothy Beaumont.

The Grey Lady of Glamis Castle, if she is indeed Lady Janet Douglas, was the sister of Archibald Douglas, the 6th Earl of Angus, who was responsible for imprisoning King James V at a young age.

The 6th Earl was widely recognized as Scotland's ruler during that time, but when King James escaped captivity in 1528, Archibald fled to England.

King James hated Archibald as well as most associated with him, including Janet. When Janet's husband died, James saw an opportunity and had the widow arrested for witchcraft. Around this time, witchcraft was considered a capital crime.

With the study of witchcraft being so serious, this resulted in Janet being burned at the stake, suggestively triggering the start of the hauntings and the spirit known as the Grey Lady of Glamis Castle.

Reports from visitors and staff claim that they've seen the grey ghost wandering the eerie halls of the castle. Tour guides say that no matter who the visitors are, not a single person will sit in the Chapel chair, known as the "ghost chair" that Lady Janet Douglas once used.

	With the dark history of her death from the false accusations of witchcraft, it's not wonder her spirit still roams the halls of the Scottish marvel. **The Lady with no tongue** Another famous ghost is the Lady with no tongue. It's unclear who she is or what happened to her, but she has been frequently seen standing at a barred window in the castle as well as pointing to her wounded face and her lack of a tongue.
Notes	There have been literally hundreds of reports from unconnected visitors who share the same description of sightings, leading many researchers to believe the ghosts of Earl Beardie and the Lady of Glamis are real and are still very much haunting the grounds.

Hy-Brasil

Date	14th Century
Location	Unknown
Type	Phantom Island
Quantity	1
Evidence	Reports, Voyages, Eye-Witness
Description	The vanishing island of Hy'Brasil is one that has driven researchers and explorer crazy with the lack of answers and the developing mysteries over the centuries. Also called Bracile, Hy'Brazil, Brazir, Hy'Breasil and Hy-Breasal (which means "High King of the World" in tales of Irish Folklore), Hy'Brasil is a phantom island that was also given the name "The Promise Land". Though there is far more evidence and reports surrounding it than there was for Atlantis, it seems to have fallen into the realm of Irish myth despite many people finding, seeing, and even visiting the island over the centuries. Hy'Brasil was said to be located about 200 miles off the west coast of Ireland in the Atlantic Ocean. It was described as two face-to-face islands with a narrow channel of water running through the middle. Many people visited the

island and it was present on maps from 1325 to the late 1800s when it was removed because its location couldn't be verified.

Multiple stories have circulated throughout Europe for centuries. Some say it was the home to an advanced culture or civilization, while others claim it was a promise land for saints.

Others say the only resident there was a strange old man, described as a "magician" or "wizard" who lived in a large stone castle and the only other inhabitants being large black rabbits. There are other claims of a civilization who were able to move objects with music and Irish folklore claims that the island was shrouded in fog and was only visible for one day every seven years.

Unknown date

Saint Barrind and Saint Brendan were reported to be the first to find the island on their respective voyages. Both have a matching description of Hy'Brasil as well as its location. It was given the nickname "The Promise Land" afterwards, likely because of the two Saints who founded it.

1325

The earliest written indication of the island was from a 1325 map by the Genoese cartographer, Angelino Dulcert, where the island was named

"Bracile".

1375

Half a century later it appeared in the Catalan Atlas in which showed it as two separate islands of the same name, "Illa de brasil".

1436

Again in 1436, it appeared on the Venetin Map by cartographer Andrea Bianco, where it was named "Sola De Brasil".

1480s

With all the mystery and the confusion of its actual location, subsequent voyages set off in the 1480s to try and locate it so they could verify and mark down its exact location for mapping. This failed and the island couldn't be found despite multiple efforts.

1497

In 1497, a Venetian explorer by the name of John Cabot reported finding the island on his voyage. There's not much information on what happened afterwards, but it was the last reported sighting of Hy'Brasil for years.

1595

In 1595 it appeared on the Abraham Ortellius Map of Europe and the Europa Mercator Map.

1674

In 1674, a man named John Nisbet claimed to have spotted Hy'Brasil on his voyage from

France to Ireland. He reported sailing through a thick fog before realizing his ship was dangerously close to rocks that were bordering the island. They anchored the boat and Nisbet sent some of his men off in a row boat, who spent the whole day exploring the island.

There's two conflicting stories about his origin and how many men rowed to the island. One story claims that Nisbet sent three men to the island while another says it was four, though this may have just been a confusion of him joining the three men to become the fourth. There are also articles that claim he was an Irish explorer, but he was in fact a Scottish explorer on a voyage to Ireland.

The men returned with gold and silver that they claimed to have been given by a "wise old man" who lived on the island. It was said that he lived alone on the island in a large stone castle and was described as a "mysterious magician". The only other inhabitants on the island were large black rabbits.

A follow-up expedition was led by captain Alexander Johnson who also claimed to have found the mysterious island, verifying all of Nisbet's claims.

1865

Following Nisbet and Johnson's expeditions, the island would become a ghost again and map-makers started leaving it off of most nautical maps. Its last map inclusion was in 1865 when it was simply noted "Brazil rock".

1872
Allegedly, Robert O'Flaherty and T.J Westropp found the phantom island in 1872 and Westropp claimed he had visited the island on three previous occasions. Captivated, he decided to take his family to get a first- hand look at it up close on another trip. Upon arriving in the area, they sailed into a thick fog. When it cleared the island revealed itself from behind the fog, but as they sail towards it, the fog brushed over their view of the island and when it cleared, the island had completely vanished.

1980
No one has seen the island since 1872 and as of 2021, that hasn't changed, but after a century of silence, the resurrection of Hy'Brasil began when in 1994, Sergeant Jim Penniston's decoded the binary from that he claims was burned onto his mind in 1980 after touching an unidentified vehicle during the Rendlesham Forest UFO incident before it took off at speed he noted as "impossible".

When decoded by an expert, the binary code included the co-ordinates of Hy'Brasil's suspected location. Since then it has become one of the biggest unsolved mysteries of our time and has captured the imagination of many mystery and UFO and researchers.

	Today, Hy'brasil isn't included on any maps, nor is there anything but ocean when you search for it on Google Earth. Now it just lives on as one of the biggest mysteries of all time..
Notes	If the disappearing phantom island is allocated to something otherworldly, it could show up again in the future and it could be linked to anything in the realm of paranormal or an advanced civilization.

Loftus Hall

Date	14th Century
Location	Wexford, Ireland
Type	Haunting
Quantity	Multiple
Evidence	Reports, Eye-Witness, Photographs
Description	The Loftus Hall is a twenty-two bedroom mansion located on the Hook Peninsula in County Wexford, Ireland. It's a large house constructed on the site of the Redmond Hall; the home of the Redmond family since 1350. Alexander Redmond died in the house, after which his family were evicted by Oliver Cromwell's soldiers and then the house was sold to Nicholas Loftus. The locals say Loftus Hall was haunted by a young woman's ghost, as well as the devil. It's regarded as the most haunted house in Ireland. The building's structure and surrounding landscape truly fits the stereotype of a haunted house. It's the unexplained mysteries and the ghost tales that have made the Loftus hall one of the most talked about haunted places in Ireland.

It all comes from the life and death of Anne Tottenham whose ghost is said to be haunting the hall.

Legend has it that at the time when the Tottenham family were the occupants of the house they received a stranger during a storm and gave him shelter in their home. The stranger stayed in the house for weeks. It was during this period that Anne Tottenham, who was a young woman at the time, grew fond of him and they spent a lot of time together.

One evening, a card game was being played and Anne bending down to pick a card looked under the table where she discovered the mystery man had cloven hoofs and not regular feet. As this happened, the man transformed into a ball of fire and shot up through the roof with the events leaving Anne in a state of trauma which she never recovered from. It's this story that made people refer to the man as the devil.

Anne was locked in the tapestry room where she remained silent for years until she died. After her death, the servants reported seeing a dark mysterious figure roaming the halls at night.

The family hired several clergymen including Father Thomas Broaders who finally succeeded in exorcising the hall. Although there are several accounts of the story that claim he was unable to exorcise the tapestry room where Anne died.

	The hall is now open for public visitation and it serves as a tourist attraction. It was reopened in 2012, since then people have claimed to have different disturbing experiences including a boy who claims to have seen Anne's ghost in one of his pictures taken from the hall. The hall was also used as location to shoot the horror movie, The Lodgers.
Notes	Many families lived in the property throughout the centuries and there could be many more ghosts that are responsible for the many hauntings and apparitions that have been spotted and even photographed.

Bhangarh Fort

Date	15th Century
Location	India
Type	Curse, Haunting
Quantity	1+
Evidence	Reports, Eye-Witnesses
Description	Surrounded by dense forrest and a wealth of unexplained phenomena, Bhangarh Fort is said to be the most haunted place in India, so much so that the Archaeological Survey of India have prohibited entry after sunset. The fort was built by Bhagwent Dasfor his son Madho Singh in the 17th century, Legend states that Baba Balunath allowed the construction of the fort under the condition that any of the buildings should not cast a shadow over his shrine. He stated that if the condition was broken, Bhangarh will be cursed and the village will be destroyed. Once Prince didn't stick to this and constructed a building that blocked sun llight to the shrine, resulting in the curse being triggered. Another legend states that a man by the name of

	Singhia fell in love with the princess of Bhangarh, Rani Ratnavati. Singhia supposedly put a love spell on an oil and sent it to the princess as a gift, but Ratnavati was well versed in the practice of Black Magic, resulting in the oil being returned and Singhia dying a painful death. Before his death, he was said to curse Bhangarh. Over the years, there have been numerous reports of injuries and even death, said to be a result of the curses.
Notes	There's been sightings of apparitions, witches and other unexplained phenomena that has caused the area to be completely restricted after dark.

The Dancing plague

Date	July, 1518
Location	France
Type	Unexplained, Possession
Quantity	Multiple
Evidence	Eye-Witnesses
Description	The dancing plague of 1518 was an unexplained event that saw a large number of people literally dancing themselves to death. Occurring in Strasbourg, Alsace, which is now modern-day France, the outbreak began in July 1518 with a woman spontaneously dancing in a street in Strasbourg. After collapsing from exhaustion, she took a break before resuming her dance frenzy. She danced for days and within a week, she was joined by another 30 people who uncontrollably danced with her despite injuries and exhaustion. Authorities were notified and attended the scene. Civil and religious leaders came to the conclusion that more dancing was the cure, thus setting up guildhalls, musicians and professional dancers to prolong the unexplained phenomena.

| | This decision only grew the problem and saw around 400 people join the uncontrollable dancing over the following weeks.

By September, the compulsive dancing started to diminish with many as many as 15 deaths a day at the peak.

Explanations for the dancing plague of 1518 consisted of the victims being possessed by a supernatural force, however 20th century research into the mystery suggests it could have been food poisoning from rye flour in bread that contained a fungal disease which was known to cause convulsions.

American medical historian, John Waller, shared his thoughts on the plague over several papers and suggested the dancing plague was a form of mass psychogenic disorder. |
| Notes | Some claimed that the people were possessed and even though the food poisoning theory is a possibility, the case is still unsolved. |

Fort Santiago

Date	17th Century
Location	Manila, Philippines
Type	Haunting
Quantity	1+
Evidence	Physical contact, Footsteps, Eye-Witnesses
Description	The most haunted place in the Philippines is widely regarded as Fort Santiago. A defense fortress built in 1593 by Spanish navigator and governor Miguel Lopez de Legazpi for the new established city of Manila. Located in Intramuros, Fort Santiago is considered one of the most important historical sites in the capital and saw a national hero, Jose Rizal, spend his final days there before his execution by firing squad in 1896. He is one of the ghosts said to haunt the grounds today with footsteps heard of him walking his route to the execution chamber. During World War II, the Japanese Imperial army took over the fort and used the prisons, dungeons, and storage cells to house thousands of people there during the Manila massacre (Rape of Manila).

During the battle of Manila, the U.S army advanced into the capital in order to drive Japan out. Civilians were violently murdered with their bodies being totally mutilated, over 400 women and young girls were raped, and massacres in schools and hospitals were also carried out by the frustrated Japanese. The battle brought the city to rubble.

It's difficult to know exactly how many people died there, but the Manila massacre saw between 100,000-500,000 deaths in total, giving it a foundation for paranormal activity. The dungeons of the fort saw around 600 American prisoner of war soldiers die of suffocation and hunger after being held in such as small enclosed area in poor conditions.

With such a violent history and an enormous amount of deaths caused by inhumane acts, is it any wonder Fort Santiago is considered the most haunted place in the Philippines?

Visitors have reported voices and screams of pain which may be due to the many people who were tortured to death there. Others have even reported being touched by unseen forces and there have been many visitors reporting seeing apparitions.

If you walk the route of Jose Rizal on the way to his execution, which is outlined at Fort Santiago by metal footprints designed on the floor, you can sometimes here footsteps of his ghost

	walking the path over and over again. Fort Santiago stands as the most haunted place in the Philippines and is open for the public to visit.
Notes	I personally visited the Fort when I was living in the Philippines. It's good a bitter sweet history, but I didn't witness any paranormal activity on my visit.

The Castle of Good Hope

Date	17th Century
Location	Cape Town, South Africa
Type	Haunting
Quantity	Multiple
Evidence	Reports, Eye-Witnesses
Description	The Castle of Good Hope or Cape Town Castle is a bastion fort built in 1667 in Cape Town, the oldest city in South Africa. This astonishing building initially served the purpose of a replenishment station for ships passing the treacherous coast around the Cape on long voyages between the Netherlands and Indonesia. For those who first settled in there, it was a relaxation station for ship personnel, but to the residents of the community, it was a nightmare; it has the most ghosts in South Africa. The fortress housed a church, bakery, different workshops, living quarters, and cells, amongst others. In 1936, the Castle of Good Hope was officially declared an historical monument, the first site in South Africa to be so protected by walls, in case of an attack.

A romantic ghost was reported to have haunted the castle; her curly-haired ghost has been known to appear at parties in the castle to honor distinguished guests. She was believed to be Lady Anne Barnard, who had lived in the castle for five years in the 1700s.

In 1915, an unidentified figure was reported to have wandered in the building, it was observed to have jumped over the high walls, and many claimed it was a ghost. This strange visitor haunts the castle and vanishes at the last instant.

More frequently, unexplainable footsteps have been heard in the same area of the castle which was believed to be the same ghost who rings the castle bell from time to time.

There' also a horrifying fact that came to light of a guard who committed suicide a century ago by hanging himself with the bell rope.

Some tourists also reported seeing a wild black dog that attacks visitors, but mysteriously disappears into the thin air. Voices of people arguing and shuffling were also heard from an underground chamber that was used for torturing, while lights went off in the dungeon without explanation.

The Castle of good hope is a place full of many fairy tales and fascinating experiences which will make a good adventure for intending visitors.

	Today, the Castle of Good Hope is a museum which houses the William Fehr collection of Africana, accompanied with a collection of ghosts.
Notes	---

The Catacombs of Paris

Date	17th Century
Location	Paris, France
Type	Haunting
Quantity	Multiple
Evidence	Reports, Eye-Witnesses
Description	The catacombs are a bone-chilling labyrinth of haunted tunnels that sit below the streets of Paris and are considered to be one of the most haunted and eerie places on the planet.
	In the 17th century, at the end of the second wave of the Black Death pandemic, Paris' cemeteries were overflowing to the point corpses were uncovered from overcrowding. Business owners in the city started to complain about the strong smell of rotting flesh, however nothing was done until 1780 when rainfall caused one of the walls to collapse, spilling corpses into a neighboring property.
	With nowhere to put all the bodies, Paris resulted to moving the bodies to a maze of 13th century tunnels that sat beneath the streets of the capital city.
	After moving skeletal remains down into the

| | catacombs, the cemeteries began to empty out, but it took the city twelve years to move all the bones into the former quarry tunnels.

There are said to be over seven million bones that were moved there with some of the skeletal remains dating back as far as 1,200 years. Paris were moving bones into the catacombs until 1860. With this many skeletal remains, is there any wonder it's considered one of the most haunted places in the world?

The catacombs is open to the public today with about a mile of explorable tunnels that takes 45 minutes to walk through. The entrance is located in Paris' 14th arrodissement, at 1, avenue du Colonel Henri Rol-Tanguy. The tunnels are open from 10am to 5pm Tuesday-Sunday and you can go into the catacombs for a few euros.

The catacombs earned its spot as one of the most haunted places in the world and in 2014 a found footage style movie, *As Above, So Below*, was released. |
|---|---|
| Notes | There's no need to explain that there have been many reports of paranormal activity down there. |

Witchcraft Book

Date	1685
Location	Scotland
Type	Witchcraft
Quantity	Multiple
Evidence	Book, Charges
Description	In 2020, a book was released on the internet for the public, but it wasn't your ordinary bathroom read, it was a 350 year old witchcraft book that published the names of potential witches as well as where they lived. It was written during the 17th century when the persecution of witches was rife in Scotland. There's also note of the witches' confessions in the book. Though many were accused and even lost their lives after being labeled a witch, many of them were actually practicing medicine. However, if the medicine testing failed, they would typically be accused of the dark arts.
Notes	Most people accused were women, some 75% or higher, but there were some men included. The book is called "The Names of Witches".

Edinburgh Vaults

Date	1788
Location	Egypt
Type	Haunting
Quantity	Multiple
Evidence	Reports, Eye-Witnesses, Spirits, Physical
Description	The haunted Edinburgh Vaults, also known as the South Bridge Vaults were constructed in the late 1700s and completed by 1788 in Edinburgh, Scotland. The tunnels and chambers have cemented their legacy in the paranormal community for being haunted, and with good reason. In the early days, the vaults were used to house workshops and a place for other tradesman such as cobblers. The space was also used for these tradesmen to store their tools and supplies. After about 30 years of operating, the vaults attracted the homeless and crime and some of the taverns transitioned into illegal gambling dens and whiskey distilleries. Allegedly corpses were also stored there by bodysnatchers. The vaults became a slum for murder and poverty.

Though much debate surrounds the theory that the Burke an Hare murders took place there, no evidence can support the two ever used the vaults during their 16-person murder spree in 1828.

By the 1820s, most of the businesses packed up shop and Edinburghs poorest moved in, living with poor air conditions and a damp murky shelter from the outside world until around 1860 when most were said to move out as well. For over 100 years, the vaults were abandoned and forgotten.

Paranormal investigators actually consider this the most haunted place in the world.

The vaults are said to be home of many spirits belonging to those who were inhumanely murdered in previous years.

There have been a mountain of the usual paranormal reports over the years and Amanda Bartlett shared her experience of the haunted vaults with reports of an unseen force pulling a jacket.

One of the most famous ghosts is said to stalk visitors. Known as Mr. Boots, he's a shabby, tall man who seems to keep himself situated at the back section of the vaults. He's been known to throw stones at visitors and many visitors have heard his footsteps following them as they

	explore the dark chambers and corridors.
Notes	This is one of Scotland's most haunted places, competing for the top spot with Greyfriars Kirkyard and Glamis Castle.

Hellfire Caverns

Date	1752
Location	England
Type	Satanic Worship, Haunting
Quantity	Multiple
Evidence	Reports, Photos, Eye-Witnesses
Description	When researching the most haunted place in England, the haunted Hellfire Caverns may not show up at the top of the list, but maybe they should. The haunted Hellfire Caverns are a labyrinth of man-made tunnels that extend quarter of a mile underground. They were built between 1748 and 1752, deep beneath the West Wycombe Hills by Sir Francis Dashwood, the founder of the infamous Hellfire Club. The caverns were kept secret at their time of construction and were said to be used for Pagan rituals and devil worship. Meetings occurred twice a month and there were many rumors of black magic and satanic rituals in circulation during the life of the club. If true, it could connect them to another haunted site in England, the Ancient Ram Inn.

The Inn was built over an ancient Pagan burial ground and is said to have spiritual energy fed to it from Stonehenge through the Ley lines. Geographically, the haunted Hellfire Caverns are in the same proximity as the Ancient Ram Inn is with Stonehenge. The three locations actually form a bit of a triangle, which you can see here:

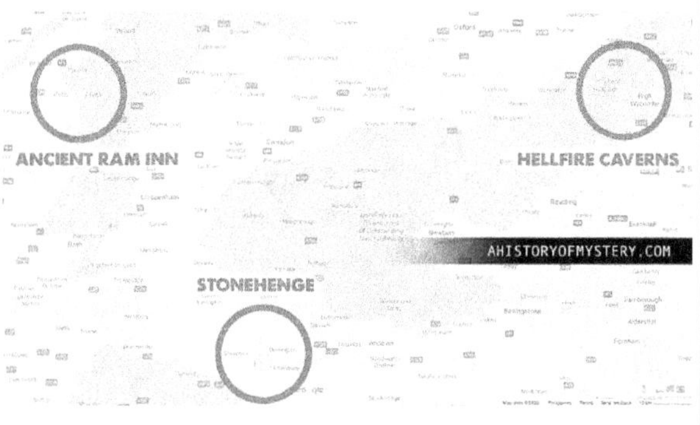

With the caverns being directly on top of Ley lines and the similarity of Pagan history like the Ancient Ram Inn, that's almost enough to justify it being haunted on its own, but there's far more to the man-made tunnels.

When entering the haunted Hellfire Caverns from above, it may take a few moment for your eyes to adjust from the sunlight outside to the dark and dimly-lit tunnel system.

As well as a collection of eerie tunnels and chambers hidden under the ground, there's also the ghosts that haunt the historic site.

	One such ghost is said to be that of a young girl in a wedding dress that was allegedly lured into the tunnels many years ago and was then stoned to death. Her apparition has been spotted by many visitors. Another is that of Paul Whitehead, a prominent member of the Hellfire club who is said to still haunt the tunnels. There have been many sightings and some have even caught photographs of unexplained apparitions while exploring the caverns. These two as well as the collection of other unexplained sightings of apparitions and paranormal occurrences, along with the Pagan and satanic history and possible connection to the Ley lines solidifies the haunted Hellfire Caverns as a credible location for paranormal research.
Notes	---

Beechworth Lunatic Asylum

Date	1867
Location	Beechworth, Victoria, Australia
Type	Haunting, Apparitions
Quantity	Multiple
Evidence	Reports, Eye-Witness, Cold spots
Description	Beechworth Lunatic Asylum in is located in Beechworth, Victoria and is considered the most haunted place in the whole of Australia.
	Operating from 1867-1995, it was built on Beechworth Hill with the belief that the altitude would rid patients of their illness, but very few ever made it out alive.
	Originally known as the Mayday Hills Lunatic Asylum, this isolated building sits on 106 hectares of farmland, designed to be completely self-sufficient with a pig farm, fields, stable and barn.
	Beechworth saw thousands of patients over the years, but when they died, they didn't really leave. Their troubled ghosts still haunt the

building today.

With medication not being developed until the 1950s, the doctors would restrain the patients with shackles and straightjackets. Many even received electric shock therapy in hopes of curing them.

During one session, the entire patient population were subjected to electric shock therapy so it's not surprising that most of the paranormal activity happens in the rooms were these experiments occurred.

Over the years, the ghost stories have poured in and visitors have reported many different experiences from footsteps creeping up behind them when no one is there, to doors slamming and shadowed figures appearing in various parts of the asylum.

People have also reported the stench of rotting flesh. This actually has some substance to it because one patient was found dead in a tree. He had been there so long that his leg had fallen off and was discovered by a dog.

Other reports are rooms turning ice cold. The ghost of a man in the gardens. Among many others.

It's possible to visit this iconic paranormal hotspot. The Australian "Asylum Ghost Tours" offers such a service. You can experience the

	ghost tour, the paranormal tour, a historic tour and special events, including spending the night at Beechworth Lunatic Asylum.
Notes	---

Bobby Mackey's

Date	1850
Location	Wilder, Kentucky, USA
Type	Haunting, Satanic Worship, Demonic, Murder
Quantity	Multiple
Evidence	Possession, Eye-Witnesses
Description	Bobby Mackey's has said to be haunted for about 40 years and is one of Kentucky's primary locations for paranormal investigators. Today, Bobby Mackey's Music World is an active nightclub in Wilder, Kentucky with country music, line dancing, a mechanical bull and regular ghost tours. Yes, you read that correctly. The haunted building has ghost tours outside of the nightclub hours which has earned popularity from the building's incredibly dark and sinister past. The club stands on the same site that was open as a large slaughter house and meat packing facility in 1850 and operated until the 1890s. At that point there was said to be much sinister activity there. There was said to be a Satanic cult that performed dark rituals around the building's well that was previously used to store the blood and

guts of the slaughtered animals during its operations. The well may have even been used to dispose of human corpses after sacrifices.

Mackey's was claimed to be a place of darkness in the late 1800s and early 1900s and a place of secret meetings where humans were murdered for ritualistic purposes.

In 1896, Scott Jackson, a student of the Ohio College of Dental Surgery, urged his girlfriend, Pearl Bryan, to come up to Cincinnati where he would perform an abortion with the help of his room mate, Alonzo Walling, but unsurprisingly the operation went wrong and the two men needed to cover their tracks in order to avoid a murder charge.

In hopes of their failed operation not being discovered, they surgically removed Pearl's head and left her body in a field just two miles from the slaughterhouse.

They were caught out after forensics traced the murder back to them because they left Pearl's shoes on, otherwise they would have gotten away with it. Whilst Alonzo was facing the gallows, he swore to haunt the area forever and Jackson had ties to a Satanic cult and Pearl's head may have been used for one of the dark rituals that were held near the well of the slaughterhouse.

There's no telling how many human rituals were

carried out at the slaughterhouse or what exactly happened there, but the cult operated in the shadows and Satanic worship, human rituals and sacrifice are not something shared with the outside world.

The building was actually demolished in the early 1900s and the site was bare for two decades, likely harboring the spirits of the victims until the 1920 when a new casino and nightclub was built there.

After mob interference who tried to muscle in on the casino, it shut down and reopened as a nightclub in the 1950s. The daughter of the new owner, Johanna, fell in love and fell pregnant by a singer there, who she intended to run off with, but her father had the singer killed.

This led Johanna to poison her father and then take her own life in the nightclub's basement, not far from where the slaughterhouse's well was situated. Though the method and poison is not known, it may have been similar to the compound used by Guilia Tofana who sold poison to many wives in Italy who murdered their husbands.

After a series of shootings, local authorities were forced to close the business in 1978, but a few months later it was taken over and re-opened to become Bobby Mackey's.

The nightclub is still operating today and the

violent and dark history has subsided, but the paranormal phenomena has led it to become well-known as the haunted Bobby Mackey's and is one America's top hotspots for investigators.

There have been a mountain of reports. From a former caretaker claiming to be demonically possessed, leading them to have an exorcism performed on them by a minster, to mysterious footsteps being heard on the steps near the historic well to people seeing ghosts in many of the rooms.

There have even been two references to Pearl and Alonzo from visitors who've experienced supernatural occurrences.

Bobby's wife claims to have been grabbed round the wrists and even pushed down the basement steps by a spirit that resembled sketches of Alonzo Walling who was screaming "get out". She refuses to return to the building.

There has also been reports from many people claiming to see a headless ghost dressed in 1890s clothing which matches historic photos of Pearl Bryan. Some still believe that the building's basement hold a gateway directly to hell.

Notes	This is ranked the second most haunted place in Kentucky, only falling short of Waverly Hills.

Borley Rectory

Date	1862
Location	Essex, England
Type	Poltergeist, Physical Attacks, Haunting
Quantity	2+
Evidence	Physical, History, Eye-Witnesses, Investigations
Description	Built in Essex in 1862, the Borley Rectory has risen to the top of the list for paranormal phenomena and is considered the most haunted house in England. Reverend Henry Dawson Ellis Bull ignored warnings from the locals that the 4-acres of land was already haunted. He had a rectory built for him and his family; a gothic-style red brick building with two stories. As soon as the Reverend and his family moved into the newly constructed house, the ghostly happenings began. Starting with unexplained footsteps that followed family members both inside and outside the property. A common ghost of Borley Rectory that was sighted was said to be that of a nun, allegedly linked to the 12th century Church on the grounds. She was seen so regularly that one

area of the ground was named "The Nun's Walk".

Another terrifying ghost that became infamously linked to the legend of the rectory was the two headless spirits that pulled a large black coach with the help of four black horses; repeatedly riding past Borley Rectory and vanishing into thin air.

May 2, 1892

The Reverend died in the'"Blue Room", succeeded by his Reverend son, Henry Foyster Bull, known most commonly as Harry. The Nun's ghosts was seen far more frequently and on June 9, 1927, like his father, Harry died in the Blue Room, and his ghost has been sighted numerous times.

After standing vacant for several months, Reverend Guy Eric Smith moved in with his family. His wife discovered a mysterious brown paper package whilst she was clearing out the cupboards. What was inside horrified them.

They discovered a skull in the package and at that point, the paranormal occurrences dramatically increased.

In 1929, the family contacted the Daily Mirror newspaper to find someone who could help. Paranormal researcher Harry Price, who wrote two books supporting claims of paranormal activity, went to investigate.

Price was famous for debunking paranormal phenomena, psychic mediums and spirit photographers, but as soon as he arrived, he knew he was in deep water.

Stones and objects came flying out of nowhere, pebbles hit the house and rolled down the stairs, and spirit messages were tapped on the mirror in the Blue Room.

Several articles were written about the hauntings and ghosts of Borley Rectory, followed by a swift departure of the family on July 14, 1929.

Borley Rectory stood empty until October 1930 when the cousin of the Bulls, Reverend Lionel Algernon Foyster and his family moved in. They experienced the same unexplained paranormal phenomena, but things escalated from there.

The increasingly violent poltergeist ripped the Reverend's wife, Marianne, out of bed one night and was she slapped and had objects thrown at her. Further more, windows were smashed, heavy furniture was overturned and fires would start unexplainably as well as doors locking and unlocking. Writing would also appear on the walls for a short time and then disappear.

Harry Price once again visited the house after two unsuccessful exorcisms on the Borley Rectory and reported many more occurrences including two bottles of wine he'd purchased turning to ink and perfume respectively.

October 1935

Five years after moving in, the family left the Rectory.

Church officials decided the house would no longer be used as a rectory and for two years it stood vacant until Harry Price convinced the owners to rent it to him for a year in order to conduct in-depth investigations into the unexplained phenomena.

March 27, 1938

Price claimed to have contacted two spirits during his time there, including a Catholic Nun from France and a spirit claiming to be Sunex Amures, stating; the house would burn to the ground that night at nine o'clock and the bones of a murder victim would reveal themselves.

December, 1938

Captain William Hart Gregson purchased the Rectory. He lived there for just under a year and reported similar paranormal activity and unexplained phenomena.

February 27, 1939

Captain William Hart Gregson accidentally

knocked over an oil lantern which burned the entire house down. This was 11 months to the day after the mysterious Sunex Amures claimed the house would burned down.

1943

Harry Price returned to the ruins of Borley Rectory once more to excavate the cellar and tunnels under the property. He found two bones including the jawbone of a woman. There were also two photos taken during the demolition of the burned building. One with a brick floating in mid-air and another of a figure walking among the tombstones.

The activity decreased after the rectory's demolition and was said to be focused more in the Church and the graveyard on the grounds.

The Nun has been sighted numerous times in the graveyard and the sound of organ music can be heard playing. The Church and graveyard are still investigated by paranormal researchers to this day.

Notes	We rank this the most haunted house in the world.

Eastern State Penitentiary

Date	1829
Location	Philadelphia, Pennsylvania, USA
Type	Haunting
Quantity	Multiple
Evidence	Reports, Eye-Witnesses, Physical, Photos
Description	The haunted Eastern State Penitentiary is America's most historic prison which was in operation from 1829-1971. The building was the most expensive public structure built in the United States at the time of its completion. It's unique spoked-wheel design was considered an architectural marvel and became a framework for more than 300 prisons worldwide. Eastern State Penitentiary has housed some of the most notorious criminal in US history, including Al Capone and the infamous bank robber, Willie Sutton. The prison had strict isolation techniques which involved 23 hours a day of lockdown and 1 hour of yard time, but prisoners weren't allowed to mingle with others. Each cell has a small court yard built onto it to keep to their strict isolation

policies.

If prisoners were taken out their cell, they would have an opaque hood placed over their head to prevent them seeing any other prisoners and vice versa. This extreme isolation was designed to cause the criminals to reflect upon their crimes, designed to cause them to reform, but actually this method resulted in mental illness.

The guards also used vicious torture techniques that were handed out for the most minor disobedience, such as simply whistling or shouting to another prisoner in an adjacent cell.

One of the torture methods prisoners experienced was the iron gag. A chain device that crossed their arms behind their back with a clamp looping round to their tongue, causing any movement to rip their tongue out.

THE IRON GAG.

There were many other torture techniques including an ice bath, that caused many deaths, straight jackets, a hole under a cell block with little light and air as well as the mad chair where prisoners were strapped in so tight for days they couldn't move, restricting the flow of blood.

These techniques, plus the extreme isolation that led to mental illness saw many of the prisoners dying or committing suicide. The prison became a place of insanity and injustice, leaving nothing but destruction and tormented souls on the grounds.

Reports have flooded in of orbs, footsteps, strange noises, shadowy figures and screams of pain and suffering. Cell block 4 is regarded as the most haunted part of the prison with faces appearing behind cell doors when the rooms are empty and apparitions walking around.

One of the guards employed to maintain the area that's still open to the public has reported being grabbed so tightly by an unseen force in cell block 4 that he was unable to move or escape until he was released.

| Notes | You can now visit Eastern State Penitentiary for day tours, group tours and even hire the venue for private events. If you would like to book tickets, you can visit:

https://www.easternstate.org/ |

Hanging Coffins of Sagada

Date	1000s
Location	Egypt
Type	Paranormal Activity, Eeriness
Quantity	Multiple
Evidence	Reports
Description	With many haunted places in the Philippines, there's one place that doesn't make popular lists; The Hanging Coffins of Sagada.
	Sagada is a mountain province about 400km north of Manila, the capital city of the Philippines. There, the people have a unique ritual when it comes to burials.
	Similarly to certain groups in Indonesia and China, the elderly people of Sagada carve their own wooden coffins out of hollowed out logs unless they're already too sick and then their families will take on the responsibility.
	The dead are placed in their wooden crypts and then taken to a cave for burial. It's reported that some corpses even have their bones broken in

order to fit them in their hanging coffins.

After the kabaong, which is Tagalog for coffin, arrives at the cave in Sagada, it's not placed in the ground like typical coffins. It's either hung on the inside of the cave walls or on the outer face of the cliffs near other hanging coffins of their ancestors.

The Sagada people have been practicing their unique ritual for over 2,000 years and some of the coffins are over a century old, but the ritual is somewhat confined to the mountain province.

Over the years and with the climate, high humidity and tropical storms in the Philippines, wood just can't be sustained outside for years on end and some of the decorative coffins fall from the walls.

	The main reason for the hanging coffins was due to a belief that the higher the corpses were laid to rest, the greater the chance of their spirits reaching a higher nature in the afterlife.
Notes	There have been reports of supernatural occurrences there, but as they are few and far between, this haunted little spot that displays the dead isn't that well known in the paranormal community. It's also quite a journey to get to Sagada.

Mary Celeste

Date	November 8, 1872
Location	Atlantic Ocean
Type	Unexplained, Supernatural, Curse
Quantity	1
Evidence	Ship, Missing Persons
Description	The Mary Celeste is the most famous real-life ghost ship that disappeared with its crew and become one of the greatest unsolved mysteries of all time. Built in 1861 in Nova Scotia, Canada, it was originally named "Amazon". It was a dual-masted wooden sailing ship and may have always been destined for doom. During its maiden voyage, the captain of the ship died of pneumonia after repeatedly coughing up blood whilst giving orders to the crew. In 1867, the Amazon ran aground in Cow Bay off the coast of Nova Scotia. Not long after the ship was repaired it got into another collision with a ship in the English Channel. Seemingly the shipped was cursed and in November 1868, it was sold to Richard W.

Haines, an American mariner from New York who renamed the cursed ship Mary Celeste and made several structural changes to make sure it was sea-worthy.

It was finally purchased by Benjamin Spooner Briggs who kept the name and was the person the ship belonged to before it and its crew vanished without a trace.

On November 8, 1872, the Mary Celeste set sail from New York, bound for Genoa, Italy with ten crew on board, but the ship never arrived. The ship was also carrying 1,700 barrels of alcohol.

On December 4, 1872, just one month after the ship had gone missing, it was discovered by a British vessel, Del Gratia, just off the coast of the Azores Islands in the middle of the Atlantic Ocean.

What's strange is that the ship wasn't discovered with the crew hanging out 930 miles west of Portugal drinking a few bottles of rum. The ship was free-sailing erratically and there were no crew on board (according to the reports of David Morehouse, captain of the Dei Gratia).

Morehouse and his men then boarded the ship and despite the sound of unexplained creaking floorboards, which would be typical for a wooden ship rolling over waves, the ship was silent.

Most people's initial thought would jump to

concluding the mystery of the ghost ship and attributing it to pirates, but not a single piece of cargo was taken, nor any of the valuables.

Here's where it gets stranger. Along with nothing missing, there was a life-boat that was unaccounted for and a fray rope trailing the ship.

There was 3.5 feet of water in the hold which could have been due to a broken water pump, but after inspection of the ship's navigational equipment and captain records, it seemed nothing went wrong and the ship had been sailing for 11 days without anyone to guide it.

Some of the men from the Dei Gratia stayed on board the Mary Celeste and the two ships sailed back to Europe. Once they arrived, Morehouse contacted the Attorney General in London, Frederick Solly-Flood.

The reason being, under maritime law a derelict ship must be examined before it can be claimed by the discoverers. Three months later, the attorney General concluded there was no foul play on the part of the Dei Gratia crew and they were rewarded with the ship.

There have been many theories over the years, some very plausible and some less plausible, ranging from sea monsters to pirates to abandoning the ship and being lost to the ocean.

	The mystery of the Mary Celeste ghost ship remains unsolved to this day because each theory still leaves unanswered questions.
Notes	If it was pirates, why was the alcohol and valuables left on board? It's difficult to conclude what happened to something from so long ago with such little to go on, but here are a few possibilities; As mentioned by Smithsonian, the ship could have been as much as 120 miles off course. If this was discovered by the crew early, they may have abandoned ship and attempted to turn back, at which point they may have been sucked under by the current and died at sea. Alternatively, they could have abandoned ship due to the water leak and assumed they needed to escape before the ship sank, leading them to the same fate of being claimed by the sea. The only other possibility is that there was foul play involved, which opens up many more possibilities. One thing we do know is that a row boat was missing so at least someone tried to escape from the Mary Celeste. Maybe one of the crew murdered the others and threw their bodies overboard and then sailed off to land and actually survived, but was never discovered? This seems plausible, but the mystery will likely remain unsolved unless

someone wants to take on the task of scouring
over a million square miles of ocean to find any
evidence of the missing crew which is likely
buried deep below the sea bed surface.

New Mexico Penitentiary

Date	1885
Location	New Mexico, USA
Type	Haunting, Unexplained Phenomena
Quantity	Multiple
Evidence	Reports, Eye-Witness, Smells
Description	Just 700 miles North East of the haunted Yuma Prison in Arizona is the New Mexico State Penitentiary which many consider the most haunted place in New Mexico. The areas of the prison where the most unusual phenomena is reported are Cell Blocks 3, 4, the toolroom and the laundry room. The Penitentiary of New Mexico (PNM) or New Mexico State Penitentiary as it is also known is a men's maximum-security prison located in unincorporated Santa Fe County, 15 miles (24 km) south of central Santa Fe. It's operated by the New Mexico Corrections Department. Opened in 1885, the New Mexico State Penitentiary had been authorized by Congress since 1853. Before it moved in 1956, there had been riots; the first occurring on July 19, 1922 and the second on June 15th, 1953.

In 1980, Cell Block 4, at the far northern end from the Control Center, was the scene of one of the most violent prison riots in the correctional system's history in the United States.

The riot began with many of the prisoners intoxicated from homemade liquor they brewed inside the prison. Over two days, 33 inmates were killed and 12 officers were held hostage by prisoners who had escaped from crowded dormitories located at the southern end from the Control Center.

Men were brutally butchered, dismembered, decapitated, hung up on the cells and burned alive. By mid-afternoon, Sunday, 36 hours after the riot had begun, heavily armed State Police officers accompanied by officers from the Santa Fe Police Department entered the charred remains of the prison.

An unusual phenomenon was reported by corrections officers and national guardsmen who use the facility for training. Commonly reported things are the human shaped shadows and the burning flesh smell. Such occurrences have been witnessed since 1981 and has continued into the present day. The tool room and laundry room were known for having these spectral occurrences.

Cell Block 3 was the maximum security ward which also contains the solitary confinement cell. Reports from here includes unexplainable noises, a burning flesh or "death" smell, doors that open and close by themselves, and lights that turn on and off without any apparent cause.

Cell block 4 was the area where the "snitches" and other prisoners held in protective custody were contained. Upon entering the cell block, there are marks on the floor where rioters used power tools to decapitate the snitches and several other inmates.

The activity reported here is similar to those reported in Cell Block 3, while the commonly reported things in the laundry room are the human shaped shadows and the "burning flesh smell".

Reports from ghost hunters who've visited the place for an investigation were that the noises, especially those that are loud and sound like cell doors slamming shut are elusive, were not able to identified by any alternative explanations other than paranormal. Thus, it remains an unsolved mystery till this day and is considered to have active ghosts and paranormal activity.

Notes	---

Slaughterhouse Canyon

Date	1800s, Various
Location	Kingman, Arizona, USA
Type	Curse, Haunting
Quantity	
Evidence	
Description	Discovered in the 1800s, one of the most haunted places in Arizona is Slaughterhouse Canyon at the base of Luana's Canyon in Kingman. Originally named Luana's Canyon after a woman named Luana, it later earned the name Slaughter Canyon because of its history of murder and unexplained screams that echo at night. Luana would stay at home in a shack in the canyon with her two children while her husband went on a long trek for weeks at a time to get food and supplies for the family. When Luana's husband didn't return home one day, food started to become scarce and she refused to watch her children starve to death. Though there may be more to the truth that was

never shared, Luana was said to become psychotic from the lack of food and urban legend states that she murdered her children to end their suffering and to prevent them starving to death. Though some sources claim she was driven psychotic with the sounds of their starving screams, other say it was due to hunger.

She was also said to cut up their bodies into smaller pieces and take them to a nearby river in the canyon and release them to flow away peacefully.

This is where the story varies again. Some say she cried at the river bank until she grew weak from starvation and died while others claimed she committed suicide. Whichever is true, she did die at the now haunted Slaughter Canyon.

Many visitors have claimed that they hear screams from the haunted Slaughterhouse Canyon at night and those screams belong to the two children and Luana.

| Notes | Due to being so secluded and horseback being the most efficient form of transport, there would have been no way for Luana to get to a food source with her children.

Many reports of eerie sounds amongst other things have been reported by visitors. |

The Amityville House

Date	November, 1974
Location	Amityville, New York, USA
Type	Haunting, Poltergeist, Murder
Quantity	Unknown
Evidence	Reports, Eye-Witnesses, Physical
Description	The Amityville Horror maybe be best known as a horror movie, but it began as one of the most famous paranormal cases of all time when Ed & Lorraine Warren investigated the paranormal activity. Located in the small town of Amityville, Long Island, just outside New York City, this now-famous house inspired one of the most well-known horror series' of all time. The story began in November 1974, though the origin may date back much further, when Ronald DeFeo Jr. murdered his entire family as they slept. The 23 year old shot both his parents to death then went from room to room and murdered all four of his siblings in the same manor. DeFeo was given six life sentences and is serving his time in a New York prison. The

reason this is relevant is because after the murders, DeFeo stated that he heard voices in the house, instructing him to murder is family.

With DeFeo in jail, the house was empty for over a year until it was purchase by George Lutz and his family, but after just 28 hours their new domicile convinced them to make a swift departure. The family's claims of supernatural phenomenon and paranormal activity in the Amityville house included slime oozing out the walls, knives being thrown off kitchen counters and the recurring image of a pig-like creature with red eyes.

The Lutz family also claimed that they had seen shadowy figures wandering inside when no one was home. George said he once saw his wife levitating above the bed and was woken up at 3:15am every morning, which just so happens to be the exact time DeFeo killed his family. It's not clear whether George knew the reported time of the murders when he made the claims.

During these experiences, the Lutz family called in a local priest, but after hearing voices warning him to "get out", he promptly left the property and halted any blessing he'd planned to perform.

Almost everyone in the Amityville community heard of the paranormal activity that the Lutz family had reported, but many questioned the authenticity of the reports. The family's debt further fueled the idea that it was all a publicity

| | stunt to try and get a movie or book deal from the hoax.

The Lutz family eventually took a polygraph test to prove their story was legitimate, to which they passed. Daniel Lutz, the boy who experienced 28 nights there, says he still has nightmares about the events of the Amityville horror house.

Ed & Lorraine Warren, who were the world's best known paranormal investigators at the time were called in when things got really bad for the family, though the Amityville story has been widely discredited as a hoax.

In 1979, the story was adapted into a book titled The Amityville Horror and then a movie in 1979 with multiple remakes and whether or not the story was true, its cemented its legacy in the horror and paranormal world. |
|---|---|
| Notes | --- |

Aokigahara Forest

Date	1900s / 2000s
Location	Mount Fuji, Japan
Type	Curse, Dark entities, Demons
Quantity	Multiple
Evidence	Reports, Suicides
Description	Given many names including "Suicide Forest" and "Sea of Trees", Aokigahara Forest at the base of Mount Fuji in Japan has been labeled the most haunted forest in the world. Filled with a supernatural presence, Aokigahara Forest draws local residents in and fills them with feelings of sadness, driving them to attempt suicide, many of which succeed. It's unknown why Aokigahara forest seems to have such a dark presence, but when people who are overcome with such feelings manage to escape alive, they just describe the feeling as being drawn there for an unknown reason. Local officials have even put signs in place to prevent people going off the public path and further down the off-track, warning them to re-consider their decision and think of their family

	members before taking their life. There have been hundred of mysterious suicides in the forest over the years with 105 bodies found in 2003 and more than 200 suicide attempts in 2010, of which 54 succeeded. Most victims commit suicide by hanging with the second most common way being a drug-overdose. It's said that the yearly peak of the suicide happens in March, which is the end of the fiscal year in Japan. Aokigahara gained international notoriety from the mysterious supernatural activity, so much so that a movie titled *The Forest* was made, using the forest as the inspiration for the Hollywood blockbuster. There have even been photographs taken from tourists and ghost hunting from within the "do not enter" advisory area of the forest with faces, shadows and apparitions captured, but the validity of the photographs has not been verified. Many ghost hunters have been to the forest with their video cameras for their Youtube channels, but few have caught more than an eerie vibe. Still, Aokigahara forest stands as one of the most haunted locations on earth and has claimed the most lives of any forest directly linked to dark supernatural energy.
Notes	Aokigahara Forest is one of the highest death

	locations linked to paranormal activity.

ByBerry Mental Asylum

Date	1907
Location	Philadelphia, Pennsylvania, USA
Type	Haunting, History
Quantity	Unknown
Evidence	Eeriness, Mistreatment, Haunting
Description	Philadelphia is the home of a dilapidated, overcrowded, undermanned mental hospital known as Byberry Mental Asylum. The primary buildings were constructed between 1907 and the mid-1920s, and the newer buildings were constructed between 1940 and 1953. The facility included over fifty buildings such as male and female dormitories, an infirmary, kitchens, laundry, administration, a chapel, and a morgue. What started out as a working farm for a few unstable patients at a time in 1903 eventually grew into a multi-building campus for the mentally ill. Although it relieved overcrowding from the other mental facilities in the area, the hospital's population grew so fast that it couldn't entice enough staff to work there, quickly exceeding its

capacity.

A national survey of institutional care of the mentally ill reported that Byberry had over 4,500 inmates, while its rated capacity was 2,500 in 1934, the peak patient population reached over 7,000 in 1960.

The name of the institution was changed several times during its history being variously named Philadelphia State Hospital, Byberry State Hospital, Byberry City Farms, and the Philadelphia Hospital for Mental Diseases.

It was home to people ranging from the mentally challenged to the criminally insane; a scary place where weird things occurred. Due to the understaffing, there was an extremely low ratio of hospital attendants to patients, and because of this, residents were often left unbathed and naked. Housekeeping fell behind, bedding was unwashed, and floors were sticky with urine. Instead of tending to the patients, staff put them in four-point restraints — sometimes for months at a time.

Several investigations into the conditions at the hospital at various points revealed that raw sewage lined the hallways, patients slept in the halls, and the staff mistreated and exploited patients; inhumane conditions and patient abuse were the main legacies of the Byberry mental hospital.

	Although some dedicated, caring, and hard-working staff truly cared for the patients, a number of bad employees carried out abuses that remain disturbing. On December 7, 1987, a press conference was held concerning the closing of the hospital. At this time the media were informed that the hospital was to be closed permanently by December 7, 1989. There's something haunting about standing in an abandoned place where thousands of people suffered over the course of many decades. That's the feeling one gets at Byberry, with its history of riots, abusive guards and medical testing on inmates. It is an unfathomable place to have lived.
Notes	Though there are few reports of ghost sightings, the grounds have been considered haunted for some time.

Centralia

Date	1962
Location	Centralia, Pennsylvania, USA
Type	Abandoned
Quantity	1
Evidence	Reports
Description	If you're a fan of Silent Hill, what you may not know is that it was based on real-life abandoned town named Centralia that's more bone-chilling than the movies. Originally a thriving coal mining town with around 2,000 residents, Centralia's population soon dwindled after a coal mining fire occurred, reducing the population to only around 1,000 residents in 1980 to just 63 in 1990. Today, there are just 5 residents living there, making it the least-populated municipality in Pennsylvania. The original cause for the Centralia mine fire is still up for debate, but some say it was due to trash being thrown in a landfill near an abandoned strip mine which ignited a coal vein. The coal fire spread through the coal mines beneath the town, creating a giant underground inferno that still burns today.

Centralia has been burning for 60 years and has given the ghost town a big name in the paranormal community as well as being the inspiration behind the Silent Hill franchise.

Some say it's a gateway to hell, but this is probably just due to the imagination of visitors who see the underground inferno pushing steam out the ground, giving it an incredibly spooky vibe.

Tourism has increased over the years as the idea of visiting a "ghost town" intrigued many thrill-seekers.

Centralia became even more popular during the 2020 Covid-19 pandemic as it was something for quarantined Americans to do while still adhering to the social distancing as the town is all but abandoned, though the dangers for visitors is

	still present. On April 6, 2020, Pagnotti Enterprises buried Graffiti Highway (one of the main road leading through Centralia that has an incredible display of graffiti) under truckloads of dirt due to concerns about liability as more tourists visit the area during the pandemic.
Notes	Though there are very few reports of any paranormal activity, the main attraction is the eeriness and the underground fire that makes the roads smoke from beneath.

Clark Air Base Hospital

Date	20th Century
Location	Angeles City, Pampanga, Philippines
Type	Haunting
Quantity	Multiple
Evidence	Reports, Voices, Noises
Description	The haunted Clark Air Base Hospital is situated in Angeles City in the Philippines. Constructed in the early 1900s and primarily used during World War II and the Vietnam War, Clark Air Base Hospital was a place for sick and dying soldiers during its years of operation. Similarly to the now haunted Fort Santiago in Manila, the hospital was used by the Japanese during the war, as well as Americans. The haunted hospital stayed open until 1991 when it was submerged in volcanic ash from the world's largest volcanic eruption of the last 100 years. The eruption of Mount Pinatubo occurred on June 15, 1991. Bursts of gas-charged magma exploded into umbrella-shaped ash clouds which sent the volcanic ash descending towards the valleys and

| | covered the hospital and Angeles City, which sits 20km east of the Mount Pinatubo.

The damage from the ash forced the hospital to close and it was eventually abandoned, that's when the ghost stories and paranormal phenomena began.

Ghosts of the haunted hospital

Many visitors have experience unexplained phenomena at the now haunted Clark Air Base Hospital and due to the amount of soldiers that died there, locals believe it's haunted by their spirits.

Screams, moans of pain, echoing voices and even phantom footsteps have been heard at the hospital, said to belong to the spirits of the people who died there many years ago.

Visitors and a security guard have claimed to hear a baby crying on the first floor of the building which was previously a pediatric center. Some have even claimed to see apparitions wandering the derelict parts of the decaying hospital.

Many parts of the building are still covered in volcanic ash as nature takes its course on the structure. The building is not open to the public due to the safety issues. |
| Notes | You can still negotiate your way in there to |

explore if you want to persuade the guard with a few thousand pesos. You'll have to watch out as the structure has erosion and parts of the walls and floors are very unstable.

The Enfield Poltergeist

Date	1977
Location	Enfield, London, England
Type	Poltergeist, Possession, Haunting
Quantity	1+
Evidence	Eye-witnesses, Photos, Investigations
Description	The Enfield poltergeist was investigated by the infamous Ed & Lorraine Warren and is one of the most famous paranormal cases in the world.

The case became known after a poltergeist was reported to haunt 284 Green Street, a small council house in Enfield. The paranormal activity occurred mainly between 1977-1979 and became world-famous after the Warrens investigated the claims.

The Enfield poltergeist mainly targeted two young sisters who lived there, age 11 and 13 at the time, starting in August 1977 when police got a call from a distressed single mother, Peggy Hodgson.

Hodgson claimed she had witnessed furniture moving and two of her children heard knocking sounds on an interior wall. The two children that heard the knocking were thirteen-year-old |

Margaret and eleven-year-old Janet, the same two that were targeted throughout the entire haunting.

Upon arriving at the residence, a police constable, WPC Carolyn Heeps, stated that they saw a chair "wobble and slide", but after inspecting it for wires or a prank she couldn't determine the cause of the movement. With no intruders and not really having a protocol for such an event, the police left. This was only the beginning though.

Over the next 18 months, claims of voices, loud noises, overturned chairs and thrown toys were reported, but the most bizarre was one of the children being levitated in mid-air.

There were many times during the case where 11-year-old Janet was in a trance and was recorded speaking with a deep demonic male voice, but ventriloquist Ray Alan visited the house and concluded that Janet's male voices were simply vocal tricks.

Over 30 people witnessed such events including neighbors, journalists and physics researchers. Many even witnessed one of the girls being levitated several feet off the ground and heavy furniture being thrown across the room in front of them. During one of the young girls being in a violent trance, the iron fireplace was ripped out from their bedroom wall.

	In 1979, reports came to an end, but the intriguing story spread across the world like a plague. In 1980, young Janet, who had been the main focus of the Enfield Poltergeist, spoke to ITV News to address some of the points of the hauntings. She admitted that her and her sister, Margaret, had actually been playing with a Ouija board before the paranormal activity started at their residence. In the aftermath of the events, there was much debate whether the hauntings were legitimate or a hoax. Ed & Lorraine Warren, who visited the house during 1978 in the midst of the hauntings claimed the case to be genuine and had a supernatural explanation, while others such as Anita Gregory and John Beloff were "unconvinced", claiming the events were faked for the benefit of journalists.
Notes	The Conjuring 2 movie was based on this case.

The Gates of Hell

Date	1970s / 1980s
Location	Derewezee, Turkmenistan
Type	Eerie, Unexplained
Quantity	1
Evidence	Reports
Description	Known more widely as the Gates to Hell or Door to Hell, the Darvaza Gas Crater is an eerie natural gas field that collapsed into a cavern and is now a continuous fire. In the late 1900s, geologists intentionally set fire to it in order to prevent the spread of methane gas and it has been continuously burning since then. The site was first discovered by Soviet engineers and was initially thought to be a substantial oil field site. The engineers set up drilling rigs to access the potential oil, but soon after the surveying of the site they discovered a natural gas pocket. The ground collapsed into a wide crater under the drilling rig and camp. Similarly to that of Pennsylvania's Centralia, there's an ongoing fire

that may burn forever.

Expecting poisonous gases to be released from the caverns into nearby towns, they was advised to burn the gases off to prevent danger to neighboring communities.

The gases were expected to burn off in a matter of weeks, but half a century later they're still burning and show no signs of stopping.

Though there is some debate over when the crater was discovered and set on fire, many believe it was discovered in the 1960s, which is also when it was said to collapse. While others state the gases were not set on fire until the 1980s. There are no records of the events from the Soviet or Turkmens so tracing it's origins and accurate dates proves a little tricky. Many believe it was set on fire in 1971.

The Gates of Hell are located in Dereweze, Turkmenistan, a lesser talked about country on the world map that sits above Iran and Afghanistan.

The Gates of Hell gas crater has a total area of 5,350m2. Its diameter is 69 meters (226 feet), and is about 30 meters (98ft) deep. Many claim that the crater is haunted and obviously given its Satanic name there's no surprise, but it appears that the only relation it has to the haunted community is the name from its hellfire looking

	flames.
	In April 2010, it was thought that the hole would be closed by the President of Turkmenistan, Gurbanguly Berdimuhamedow, who visited the gas crater. But in 2013, he declared the region where the crater sits in the Karakum Desert a nature reserve.
Notes	In 2019, rumors were going around that Gurbanguly Berdimuhamedow, had died, so he went on local television to disprove his death by doing doughnuts around the Darvaza Gas Crater on a motorbike.

Greyfriars Kirkyard

Date	1998
Location	Edinburgh, Scotland
Type	Poltergeist
Quantity	1
Evidence	Physical, Photos
Description	Sir George Mackenzie of Rosehaugh's mausoleum sits on the Greyfriars Kirkyard which is a grave yard in Edinburgh, Scotland and is said to be extremely haunted by MacKenzie himself. During what is now known as the Killing Time, MacKenzie was known for his elaborate torture and murder techniques, earning him the name Bloody MacKenzie. He was a member of Scottish Parliament and the council, but was responsible for carrying out the King's dirty work. MacKenzie was responsible for nearly 18,000 deaths over his 8-year reign. Eventually MacKenzie died in 1691 and was buried at Greyfriars Kirkyard in a tomb to memorialize him which has been given the name "The Black Mausoleum". Just over 300 years after his passing was the first report of any kind of mysterious happenings at Greyfriars...

It was 1998 when the hauntings began. A homeless man found his way into Greyfriars and broke into MacKenzie's tomb, likely looking for shelter as some sources state it was storming at the time.

After gaining access, he tried to open the crypt, probably in search of jewelry or anything valuable that may have been inside, but in doing so he fell through the corroded floor into a burial pit below. He was surrounded by centuries-old bones with the stench of death surrounding him. The unsuspecting homeless man climbed out the pit, escaped the mausoleum and ran off screaming into the night. He wasn't seen or heard from again.

That is what is said to have released the evil spirit of the Bloody MacKenzie. A few weeks later, two visitors reported a cold gust of air blowing them back, after which one of them had no memory due to being rendered unconscious at the entrance of the tomb. When awoken, it was discovered she had choke-like bruises around her throat as if she had been strangled by an invisible entity.

Following what is believed to be the release of MacKenzie's ghost, there have been over 500 visitors whom have suffered everything from burns, scratches, nausea, and dizziness. There are even documented pictures of these reports and one person even had their finger broken by an unseen force. There's no doubt this is one of

	the more violent poltergeists with the ability to physically harm any human they deem fit. In 1999 an exorcism was conducted at the mausoleum by Colin Grant, a minister of a church. During the exorcism to try and ward off evil spirits, he felt the presences of hundreds of tormented souls and claimed the negative energy and evil was too powerful. He left Greyfriars without completing the exorcism and mysteriously died three weeks later from a heart attack. When the exorcism was being performed, a picture was taken with what looks like a person stood looking out the window of the building that borders MacKenzie's tomb, strangely the building was derelict and no one was inside. The spirit of the Bloody MacKenzie is still a mystery and maybe he still walks the Greyfriars Kirkyard today, waiting for more visitors to come and see just how far he's willing to go.
Notes	Though most people consider the Edinburgh Vaults the most haunted place in Scotland, Greyfriars should probably take the number one spot due to the nature of the supernatural occurrences and the violence involved.

Hoia Baciu Forest

Date	1960s and later
Location	Cluj-Napoca, Romania
Type	Haunting
Quantity	Multiple
Evidence	Reports, Photos, Eye-Witnesses
Description	This haunted forest and UFO hotspot is situated in Cluj-Napoca, not far from Bran Castle in Transylvania and has far more mysteries behind it than just ghosts and spirits. Hoia Baciu forest has been called Romanian's Bermuda Triangle. Supposedly named after a shepherd that went into the forest with his flock of 200 sheep and never returned, Hoia Baciu is surrounded with mystery that scientists simply can't explain. Many who've visited Hoia Baciu forest have captured images of apparitions in the trees that shouldn't have been there and reported many other ghostly activity from unexplained lights coming from nowhere, shadows, orbs and terrifying sounds. There are some who claim to have been touched or assaulted by an unseen force. There's an area in the forest where electronic devices are known

to malfunction for unknown reasons, but after conducting tests it was revealed that there's electromagnetic interference among other anomalies that led many to believe it could be a gateway to a higher dimension or even a link to a higher more advanced civilization.

Strangely, electromagnetism is what's been the most talked about force in anti-gravity research, which is likely what an advanced civilization would use to travel so quickly and efficiently without being slowed down by the atmosphere.

There have also been very clear and verified images taken in the 1960s of unidentified disc-like crafts that elevated above the tree lines and flew off at impossible speeds.

Hoia Baciu Notorious Circle

With the potential of being connected to the paranormal world and sightings of crafts that resembled technology not in human inventory, how could this place get any more bizarre?

There's unexplained growth patterns in the trees throughout the forest, but at the center of the forest lies something more strange.

There's a large clearing where not a single plant, tree of any kind of vegetation can grow. There's no reason for it and no one can seem to explain it. This prompted a team to go into the forest and examine soil samples to try and conclude why

	nothing was about to grow in this large area which has now been labeled the "Notorious Circle". After soil samples were examined, there was absolutely no reason why vegetation isn't able to grow there and the mystery remains unsolved.
Notes	Allegedly, whilst a family were out exploring the forest with their 5-year-old daughter, the little girl ran off, suggestively into the notorious circle, but when her parents looked for her she had vanished from sight. An extensive searched was carried out by Romanian police, but the little girl had literally vanished into thin air. Some 4-5 years later, a local farmer discovered a young girl out the outskirts of the forest who was crying in distress. It was the 5-year-old girl, but she hadn't aged and her clothes were completely untarnished as if she had spent those years frozen in time and she had no recollection of the missing time. I contacted Romanian police, but was unable to verify whether or not the story is true and accurate.

Hotel del Coronado

Date	1892 / 1980s
Location	Coronado, California
Type	Haunting, Supernatural Activity
Quantity	1
Evidence	Eye-Witnesses, Reports
Description	The Hotel del Coronado sits on Orange Avenue in Coronado, California and has become somewhat of a conversation piece in the paranormal community as well as a historic unsolved murder site. Though the Hotel del Coronado is considered haunted, the paranormal activity is targeted to one specific part of the hotel, Room 3327, but let's rewind back to the 1800s where the historic hotel was the place of a mysterious crime scene. The story began on November 29, 1892 when Kate Morgan, who was in her late twenties at the time, was found dead on the beech steps of the Hotel del Coronado. Though her death was attributed to a self-inflicted gunshot wound to the head, a San Francisco lawyer, Alan May, suggested in the 1980s that her death was probably not suicide

as the bullet in her head didn't match her gun which would make the case an unsolved murder hat will probably never be concluded.

Kate Morgan's murder is still unsolved if you believe it wasn't a case of suicide, but the mystery of her ghost still lingers around the property for guests and visitors to experience.

Morgan stayed in Room 3327 for five days before her mysterious death and it's said that her ghost still wanders the hotel, primarily seen in her old guest room where she stayed in the days before her death.

Guests have reported a vast list of unexplained activity including flickering lights, inexplicable scents and sounds, phantom wind, rapid changes in room temperature, moving items, and the television turning on and off. Doors are said to randomly open and close on their own and there have been numerous occasions where visitors have heard unexplainable footsteps and voices.

| Notes | Despite all this, Kate Morgan's old Room 3327 is the most requested room by guests at the Hotel del Coronado. |

Island of Dolls

Date	1950s
Location	Xochimilco, Mexico
Type	Haunting, Spirits
Quantity	Multiple
Evidence	Dolls, Reports
Description	Islands are mostly known for their beaches, coral reefs, oasis of serenity, and beautiful sunsets. But the island of the dolls is known for something more. In the 1950s, the Island of Dolls, also known as La Isla de las Muñecas, was inhabited by a man named Julián Santana Barrera who one day found the corpse of a young little girl floating at the bank of a river close to the canal. Shortly thereafter, Barrera saw a floating doll near the canals. Most probably, the doll belonged to the girl. Feeling distraught for not being able to rescue her, Barrera believed that he could appease the spirit of the girl by hanging her doll on a tree. He soon realized that the doll was possessed by the spirit of the dead girl, claiming that it haunted him. So he continued to collect discarded dolls

	from the garbage, hanging them on tress over the entire island. In no time, the island was filled with many dolls which he claimed has the spirits of the dead child in them. On several occasions, residents of the island reported that they had heard the dolls whispering to each other, while others who were on a boat near the island said the dolls lured them to come down to the island. In 2001, after 50 years of collecting dolls and hanging them on the island, Barrera was found dead, drowned in the same spot where the girl was discovered. Many people said that the dolls, inhabited by tortured spirits, conspired to murder the old man. After his death, the area became a popular tourist attraction where visitors bring more dolls. The dolls are still on the island, which is accessible by boat.
Notes	In addition to hundreds of dolls, the island also contains a small museum with some articles from local newspapers about the island and the previous owner. There's a store and three rooms, one of which seems to have been used as a bedroom. In this room is the first doll that Julian collected, as well as Agustinita, his favorite doll. Some of the visitors place offerings around this doll in exchange for miracles and blessings, some

<table>
<tr><td></td><td>others change their clothes and maintain it as a form of worship.</td></tr>
</table>

Catacombs of Palermo

Date	1920s
Location	Palermo, Sicily, Italy
Type	Haunting
Quantity	Multiple
Evidence	Reports, Corpses
Description	When thinking of catacombs, the millions of bones buried below the streets of Paris probably come to mind, but these haunted catacombs in Italy are lesser known and equally as haunted.
	The Italian catacombs in Palermo, also known as the Capuchin Catacombs, Catacombe dei Cappuccini, Capuchin Monastery Catacombs or Catacombs of the Capuchins, are a bone-chilling display of skeletons in the the city of Palermo in Sicily. Originally designated strictly for the corpses of monks, the catacombs also became a show casing place for the rich to display and preserve the corpses of their loved ones so they could visit them.
	The catacombs consists of around 8,000 corpses and many have been preserved with advanced techniques to keep them as "fresh" as possible. One specific corpse is that of the last body that was taken there in 1920 by the name

of Rosalia at the age of just 2-years-old. The techniques kept Rosalia looking so well preserved that she's been dubbed "Sleeping Beauty".

The preservation techniques were lost for decades when the doctor who administered the secret techniques died. The process included using formalin to kill bacteria, alcohol to dry the body, glycerin to keep her from overdrying, salicylic acid to kill any fungi that may have grown and to keep the bodies' rigidity, and zinc salts were used.

The techniques worked so well that Rosalia and a few other corpses that reside at the haunted catacombs are displayed in an open crypt, complete with their hair, eyelashes and near-perfect skin.

Unlike the catacombs under the streets of Paris, the Capuchin Monastery Catacombs showcase the bodies in a much more elegant way. Though there's nearly 1,000 times more corpses under the streets of Paris and it's undoubtedly more haunted, the Italian catacombs reign supreme as a tourist attraction for those looking to find a classic display of skeletons and preserved corpses.

| Notes | --- |

Kolmanskop

Date	1000s
Location	Egypt
Type	Ghost town
Quantity	Unknown
Evidence	Reports
Description	Kolmanskop, which is Afrikaans for Coleman's Head, is a haunted ghost town in a one of Africa's southern deserts in Namibia. Situated in the Namin desert and was named after Johnny Coleman who left his ox wagon there during a sandstorm. The village was once a thriving mining village, but now stands as a tourist attraction for anyone wishing to explore this abandoned ghost town. The discovery of a diamond in 1908 was made by Zacharias Lewala who showed his superior. Realizing the region was rich in diamonds, the German miners settled there and started to exploit the diamond field, declaring it as a Sperrgebiet (German for "prohibited area"). The village was built up with German-inspired architecture. The village consisted of a hospital, school, theater, ballroom, power station, ice

factory and casino. It also saw the first x-ray station in the southern hemisphere and Africa's first ever tram.

After World War II, the area was in decline and the diamond field started to deplete. By the 1950s the village was already being neglected and was totally abandoned in 1956.

The properties in the village are now knee-deep in sand, something totally expected after nearly 70 years of being sat uncared for in the African desert.

The ghost town of Kolmanskop is a photographer and Instagrammer's heaven as it offers some spectacular shots of the buildings that appear to be consumed by the desert.

Notes	As with many abandoned villages and ghost towns, the paranormal stories follow and many believe Kolmanskop is haunted. Though the fact it is a "ghost town" may be what fueled the paranormal stories and they may in fact be no ghosts there, similarly to Ohio's Helltown and Italy's underwater Ghost town.

Ohio's Helltown

Date	1800s / 1900s
Location	Newville, Ohio, USA
Type	Ghost Town
Quantity	Unknown
Evidence	Reports
Description	The abandoned ghost town of Newville, OH is home to a small village that has been given the name "Hell Town". The surrounding region was previously known as Boston, Ohio and was founded in 1806. But when President Gerald Ford signed a bill that gave the federal government the right to expropriate the land under the National Park Services, the residents were forced to leave. The citizens who were forced out of their homes left a message on the wall of one of the houses saying "Now we know how the Indians felt". The U.S. government attached "No Trespassing" signs on the empty homes, but their plans for the park never came to fruition, turning this Native-American village into an abandoned ghost town. Over its years of being deserted, toxic chemicals

	were improperly disposed of there and in 1985 when the area was highly polluted, Rangers who visited were said to become ill and rashes appeared all over their bodies. A church there, which was said to be built by Satanists, was suggested to fuel a little bit of the paranormal belief. An abandoned bus that sits there is also said to host a spirit that's been reported by numerous people. There are more unrealistic reports of mutants that were created due to the toxic chemicals, one said to be a monstrous snake known as the "Peninsula Python".
Notes	Much of the reports that give Hell Town its haunted reputation have actually been discovered to be false and the assumption is that the name itself has given wandering minds the belief that its haunted.

The Overtoun Bridge

Date	2005
Location	Scotland
Type	Unexplained Phenomena
Quantity	Multiple
Evidence	Reports
Description	This mysterious bridge was built in 1895 and is located in West Dunbartonshire in Scotland and has caught the attention of paranormal researchers as well as other communities since it became famous for the very strange phenomena surrounding it. In 2005, media started getting reports of people's dog mysteriously jumping off the bridge, most of which died on impact on the rocks some 50 feet below. Allegedly, the landmark has been the location of murder and attempted murder in the past as well, but nothing can explain the dogs that are seemingly possessed. Between local researchers and the media, the number of dogs that have jumped off the Overtoun bridge are said to be 300-600 with at

	least 50 dogs dying from the unexplained leap.
	The only established link to these mysterious jumps are the breed of dog. The only dogs that seem to be compelled to make the jump are long-nosed breeds, such as German Shepherds. The only explanation for these reports attributes the reason to the smell of animals in the foliage below. This does give some closure as said breed typically have a greater sense of smell. The dogs always jump from the same spot on the Overtoun bridge, though. It's also reported that the dogs jumping are only reported on bright, sunny days, but this is likely because that's the most favorable time to walk a dog.
Notes	---

Pete the Poltergeist

Date	1990s
Location	Cardiff, Wales
Type	Poltergeist, Haunting
Quantity	1
Evidence	Reports, Eye-Witnesses
Description	Known as Pete the Poltergeist or the Cardiff Poltergeist, this is a case that gained a lot of media attention in the early 90s, but has slipped into the forgotten archives since then. Pat and John Matthews were the owners of a lawn and grass cutting equipment company called Mower Services with their store down an ally, just off a main road in Cardiff. Whilst John and his team were working, they heard what sounded like stones rolling down the metal sheet roof. Assuming it was local kids trying to annoy them they went outside, but the ally was empty. After this continued to happen, the action then moved inside the workshop. Small things started to inexplicably fly across the room including small stones and bolts. There was also a spot in the corner that became extremely cold with a

strong burning smell.

Not convinced it wasn't one of the staff just playing around with his fellow colleagues, John instructed his staff to put their hands face down on a table with him. After a moment, a stone was thrown across the room at his request, then a spark plug. This confirmed to them all that there was some kind of supernatural presence there with them.

Not feeling like they were in any danger and knowing there was not much they could do about it, they accepted the supernatural spirit and even named him… "Pete the Polt", short for Pete the Poltergeist.

John and Pam called in paranormal research and university professor David Fontana who showed up unannounced to try and catch them in the act of a hoax, but as he walked in a stone flew in front of him and hit a piece of machinery.

Following his reports it turned into a media frenzy and despite the Matthews not wanting to publicize it so customers weren't scared off, the attention actually grew their business with people wanting to meet Pete the Poltergeist.

With so many eye-witness accounts due to the influx of customers, this became one of the biggest poltergeist cases of its time.

There was one occasion when Pete was

	spotted. John and one of his staff spotted a small boy sat on one of the workshop shelves, but disappeared shortly afterwards. When Mower Services outgrew its current workshop, the Matthews moved to a larger industrial space, leaving Pete the Poltergeist to haunt the next victim.
Notes	There was an unverified report that the poltergeist activity occurred in their home, but didn't following them to their new business location.

Poveglia Island

Date	1000s
Location	Egypt
Type	Curse, Haunting
Quantity	Multiple
Evidence	Reports, Eye-Witnesses, Physical
Description	Italy's Poveglia Island has a extremely dark and sinister history, but its real claim to fame is the heart-stopping paranormal activity that occurs there today. The island sits just half a mile from the architecturally impressive city of Venice. The first inhabitants arrived in the year 421 while fleeing barbaric invaders who devastated the mainland. The invaders didn't waste their time on Poveglia as it was a small island and easily defendable by its inhabitants. The Venetian government later used Poveglia Island as a quarantine zone for victims of the black plague, a deadly pandemic that swept through Europe from 1347-1351, seeing thousands of people starting to be sent there in 1348. This caused the islands inhabitants to get infected as well, causing additional casualties. In the 17th century, the second wave swept

through Europe, causing more deaths and more people were sent Poveglia, ultimately being a death sentence.

Both pandemics saw bodies burned by the thousand and it's said that 50% of the island's soil is made up from human remains that have seeped into the ground over the centuries. That's certainly a strong basis for paranormal activity, but that was just the foundations for the sinister events that came next.

In the 1800s, a poorly constructed asylum housed the mentally ill, but it was used as a place of exile rather than rehabilitation. This resulted in more deaths over the years with unethical disposing of the bodies before a mental health hospital was established in 1922.

The island's privacy and isolation provided a perfect setup for inhumane experiments. The doctor who administered these experiments could do as he pleased with the patients.

The notorious doctor took the mentally ill and performed lobotomies on them against their will. These experiments were indescribably painful with no anesthesia and little attention given to any kind of sanitization and sterilization. He would use raw tools such as hammers, chisels and drills. He also used electric shock therapy, all in pursuit of curing mental illness, but those experiments seem to have led him down a darker path of out-right torture and murder which he conducted on patients one at a time in the island's bell tower.

The methods he used are not exactly known, but the screams of the patients could be heard across the island.

The doctor's reign of terror soon came to an end when he reported hearing and seeing ghosts himself. The story of his death has a couple of variations, but all have the same ending.

Some say he committed suicide by throwing himself off the bell tower. Another is a claim from a nurse that says he was pushed by a unseen force, while others say it was his patients that sent him plunging to his death. Some say he died on impact, but a nurse stated he survived the fall and was then suffocated by a shadowy apparition, likely the tormented soul of one of his victims.

Overall, it's not known how many people died on the island from the black plague, but it is said to be over 100,000, which is a huge number for an island of just 17 acres.

The hospital finally closed in 1968. Many articles state it was acknowledged as a retirement home, but that was due to the facility being converted to a geriatric center from 1968 to 1975. The decaying ruins are slowly claimed by greenery and the island is completely off limits to the

	public.
	The island is now a restricted area. However, visitors, either being granted access or illegally exploring, have reported paranormal activity from both inside and outside the buildings. Visitors and ghost hunters have reported shadows, noises, feelings of anxiety and unease, which isn't surprising when you consider the island's history.
	Fisherman and construction workers who attempted to restore the island's buildings have reported screams and strange noises coming from Poveglia and many have said you can hear the sounds of the tower bell ringing at night.
	In 2016, five Americans took a water taxi to the island and decided to stay the night, but were rescued by Italian emergency services when a sailboat heard them screaming in panic and alerted the authorities.
	In 2014, the *New York Daily News* reported that Poveglia and four other pieces of Italian real estate went to auction due to the declining economy. Poveglia's future is still undecided, but it still remains off limits to people today.
Notes	There was a report of people visiting Poveglia and one of the group were pushed off the side of the island and into the ocean by an unseen force.

The Italian government put Poveglia up for auction to relieve its massive public debt and found a buyer in Luigi Brugnaro, an Italian business man who paid 400,000 euros.

Unverified: Luigi has a 125 year lease on the island.

The Queen Mary

Date	1900s
Location	Multiple, California
Type	Haunting
Quantity	Multiple
Evidence	Reports, Eye-Witnesses
Description	One of the creepiest and most haunted places on earth is said to be the mysterious Queen Mary transatlantic ocean liner, now permanently docked in Long Beach, California and is used as a hotel. Since she was constructed, several employees and guests have seen ghostly figures and heard mysterious sounds. The Royal Mail Ship is a retired British ocean liner that sailed primarily on the North Atlantic Ocean from 1936 to 1967. She was laid down on December 1, 1930 by John Brown & Company in Clydebank, Scotland and was launched on September 26, 1934 by Queen Mary herself. The ship sailed on its maiden voyage on May 27, 1936. Among facilities available on board haunted Queen Mary, the liner featured two indoor

swimming pools, beauty salons, libraries and children's nurseries for all three classes, a music studio and lecture hall, telephone connectivity to anywhere in the world, outdoor paddle tennis courts and dog kennels.

The largest room onboard was the first class main dining room, spanning three stories in height and anchored by wide columns. The ship had many air-conditioned public rooms onboard. The first-class swimming pool facility spanned over two decks in height. Accommodation ranged from fully equipped, luxurious first class staterooms to modest and cramped third-class cabins.

One of the hotbeds of paranormal activity on the ship was the first class swimming pool. People have reported seeing a number of ghosts here, including a young woman in a tennis skirt walking down stairs and disappearing behind a pillar, a woman in an old wedding gown next to the pool with a little boy in a suit, and a cloud of steam appears out of nowhere along with a little girl in a blue and white dress who disappears in an instant.

Chris Wilmoth, the director of marketing at the Queen Mary, told Travel + Leisure in an email;

"The unique history of the ship allows us to offer one-of-a-kind and authentic experiences that delve into the paranormal, from evening tours and ghost investigations to overnight stays in

<table>
<tr><td></td><td>our most haunted Stateroom, B340."

It's believed these ghosts are those of people who have died on ship or once lived there. This stateroom (Stateroom B340) was a problem long before the Queen Mary opened as a hotel. In 1948, a British third-class passenger, Walter J. Adamson, passed away in the room, but the details of his death are unknown.

Later, in 1966, a woman staying in the room reported that she was woken up when the bed covers were pulled off her and she saw a man standing at the foot of her bed. She screamed and rang for the steward, but the man apparently vanished into thin air.

Years later, guests staying in the same room reported hearing someone knock on the door at midnight and saw bathroom lights mysteriously turn on. Even the hotel maids complained that they would find the bathroom water running when no one had stayed in the room for days.

Whether this historical landmark was haunted or is just a hoax, no one knows. Certainly, it's an unexplained mystery.</td></tr>
<tr><td>Notes</td><td>The hull of the ship is also said to be extremely haunted and has been explored by numerous paranormal investigators who have recorded unexplained sounds amongst other things.</td></tr>
</table>

Monte Cristo Homestead

Date	1910
Location	New South Wales, Australia
Type	Poltergeist, Haunting
Quantity	1+
Evidence	Reports, Eye-Witnesses
Description	The haunted Monte Cristo Homestead is a historic building located in Australia, but its architecture isn't the only thing that intrigues visitors. Unlike Australia's most haunted location, Beechworth Lunatic Asylum, the Homestead was a residential property, but stands up against all other contenders with its extreme hauntings. This isolated house was built in 1884 by Christopher Crawley and was handed over to his wife in 1910 when he passed away. Though his wife, Elizabeth, had been left this beautiful property she couldn't get over his death and it's said that she became a recluse, only leaving the house twice after his death until she eventually died years later from a ruptured appendix. During the time between her husband's death and hers, she converted an upper box room in

the house to a chapel and studied the bible. Elizabeth Crawley's ghost is one that is said to walk the haunted Monte Cristo Homestead and her ghost is said to be attributed to the sensation of ice cold air falling like snow.

During the house's history, other events have caused many to believe more in the paranormal activity, including unexplained noises, shadowy apparitions and orbs. There has even been notes that poltergeists are present in the building.

A maid who worked at the house was said to fall from the upstairs balcony to her death at some point in the building's history. It's difficult to fall off a balcony so it could have been attributed to one of the spirits that already haunted the property, pushing her to her death, but without knowing more details, this is purely speculation.

Either way, the death of the maid may be the cause for a common figure seen around the house that wears a dress similar to what the maid would have worn. The ghost has been primarily seen walking to the bottom of the steps where she fell.

There's also the ghost of a stable boy who allegedly burned to death in the coach house. Another is that of a ghost of a mentally disabled man known only as Harold. Legend has it that he was chained in a caretaker's cottage for four decades and shortly after being admitted to a

	mental institution, he died. His ghost has been spotted at the haunted Monte Cristo Homestead and the sound of clanking chains alerts visitors that he's close by.
Notes	---

The Pontefract Poltergeist

Date	1960s, 1970s
Location	Pontefract, West Yorkshire, England
Type	Poltergeist, Haunting
Quantity	1
Evidence	Physical, Eye-witnesses, Video, Photos
Description	Home to Europe's most violent poltergeist, 30 East Drive in Pontefract is considered one of the most haunted houses in the world with most agreeing it's also home to the most violent poltergeist in the world.
	The property was purchased in 1966 by Jean & Joe Pritchard who moved into their new home with their children Philip (15) and Diane (12).
	During the children's first summer bank holiday while the parents were away, and left Philip's auntie to watch over them, unexplained events began to unfold.
	Chalk started falling from head height to the ground, as if appearing from nowhere and slowly dropping to the floor. In an attempt to clear it up, Mrs Kelly (Philip's Auntie) went into the kitchen

and slipped on a small mysterious pool of water on the kitchen lino.

Putting her attention to the water, she started to mop it up, but as she did other small pools of water appeared in front of her and Philip's eyes. This was only the beginning...

Further inexplicable happenings came pouring in, from green foam spouting from the taps (facets) and toilet, even after the water had been shut off. Here are some of the other mysterious occurrences that took place:

–Tea dispenser activating and overflowing
-Lights that randomly turned on and off
-Potted plants ejecting themselves into the air
-Cupboards violently shaking
-Levitating objects including a solid Oak sideboard
-Jugs of milk levitating and being poured over skeptical visitors

Those were the more tolerable occurrences, but things quickly escalated starting with a sharp kitchen knife controlled by an invisible force making its way to family pictures and slashing them up. This showed the entity might have malicious intent towards the family and the events continued to prove that was true.

The family had exorcisms performed on the house to try and ward off the dark entity, but all were met with serious resistance, resulting in holy water seeping out the walls, faces being physically slapped and people pushed down the stairs by an unseen force. Fur gloves floated in mid-air, suggestively worn by the ghost who visually conducted the Christian songs which attempted to ward off the evil spirit, mocking the attempts of an exorcism.

The poltergeist become more violent after that, mostly targeting Diane. Visible bruises and scrapes to skin led to the climax when Diane's hair stood on end before being dragged backwards up the stairs by the poltergeist while she was kicking and screaming. This left Diane extremely traumatized with clearly visible finger marks around her throat.

The late 60s and early 70s saw some of the most historic paranormal events that have ever unfolded with physical harm and a supernatural force interfering with our world, witnessed by many, but formal investigation didn't begin until years after the hauntings had stopped.

A young amateur historian with an interest in Cluniac Monks decided to investigate and the hauntings were apparently caused by the ghost of a Monk who had been hung for rape during the reign of Henry VIII. This earned the ghost of 30 East Drive the name "The Black Monk Poltergeist".

There have been many recent reports of more strange occurrences at 30 East Drive which can be seen on Youtube. But one of the most rewarding investigations came from a team called Paranormal-X and you can view their discoveries at 30 East Drive using the Microsoft Skeletal Detection technology on their Youtube channel.

| Notes | The events of 30 East Drive have inspired a movie which was released in 2012, titled *When the Lights Went Out* and likely many more that took ideas from the events. |

Picture taken from 30 East Drive

Roland Doe

Date	1940s
Location	USA
Type	Possession
Quantity	1
Evidence	Reports, Exorcism, Physical
Description	Most people know of the 1973 movie, The Exorcist, and the novel before it, but what most people may not know is that it was inspired by a true story. The exorcism of Roland Doe.
	Roland Doe's real name was kept private, but the story as made public and this served as this basis for the novel and movie that followed years later.
	In 1949, Roland was 14-years-old. The occurrences started with furniture moving and other smaller objects, such as vases, levitating and flying off their own accord. Shortly after, Doe was reportedly possessed by a demon.
	An exorcism was conducted, then another by Priest Raymond J Bishop.
	During the exorcism, Doe managed to slip one of his hands out of the restraints, broke a bedspring

from under the mattress, and used it as an impromptu weapon, slashing the priest's arm open. This caused the exorcism to end prematurely.

Afterwards, the family took Roland to St. Louis in Missouri when his cousin contacted a professor at the university. Bishop spoke with Willim S Bowden, who was a priest at the college church, and he accompanied Bishop to visit Roland in his relatives' home.

During their visit, they witnessed a shaking bed, flying objects, and the boy speaking in a demonic voice. Bowdern was then granted permission from the archbishop to performRoland's second exorcism. The exorcism took place at The Alexian Brothers Hospital in St Louis, Missouri.

Priest Walter Halloran was requested to join from the psychiatric wing of the hospital. William Van Roo, a Jesuit priest, was also there to assist.

Halloran stated that during the exorcism, word such as "evil" and "hell", along with other various marks, would appear on Roland's body out of nowhere.

During the Litany of the Saints portion of the exorcism ritual, Roland's mattress began to violently shake and he broke Halloran's nose, but the exorcism was performed successfully.

Notes	After the ordeal, Roland recovered and, minus

this extremely traumatizing event, he went on to
live a normal life.

The Stanley Hotel

Date	1900s
Location	Estes Park, Colorado, USA
Type	Haunting
Quantity	Multiple
Evidence	Reports, Eye-witnesses (including Stephen King), Sounds, Photos
Description	Opened on July 4, 1909, the Stanley hotel is one of the most well-known haunted locations in America, maybe on the earth. The hotel was built in Estes Park, Colorado, which sits just outside the entrance to the Rocky Mountains National Park, as a resort for the upper class and was apparently also used as a health retreat for those who suffered of pulmonary tuberculosis. The owner recovered from the disease, but claims the hotel was never a tuberculosis retreat. The disease caused thousands of deaths over the years condemning the facilities which held the sick and dying to be haunted by the spirits. Waverly Hills is the star of the show when it comes to tuberculosis as it was considered the most haunted place in the world at one point, but

we'll get to that later.

The haunted Stanley hotel and some of its acclaimed ghosts served as inspiration for the Overlook Hotel in Stephen King's *The Shining.*

King was once a resident at the hotel before writing the novel and reportedly saw the ghosts of children playing in the hallway.

With the Stanley hotel being known for a lot of unexplained phenomena, running ghost tours seemed like a logical decision to increase revenue. Many people wanted to experience the so-called hauntings and in 2017, the Mausling family from Aurora, Colorado visited the property to do just that.

They enjoyed the ghost tour, but it wasn't until they got home that they noticed one of their photos they had taken actually contained the real-life ghost that inspired *The Shining.*

Though there has been some debate over the authenticity of the photo, and despite none of the people present noticing the ghost during the tour, the photo that was taken by John "Jay" Mausling, clearly shows a young girl walking up the stairs in clear sight of everyone. He claims the photo has not been altered in any way.

Ben Hansen, a former FBI agent and host of *Fact or Faked: Paranormal Files*, said:

If the paranormal world does exist then the Stanley hotel is undoubtedly haunted and if this photo is authentic then it may be the clearest picture ever taken of the ghost.

One of the most common ghosts comes from multiple reports of people hearing children playing in the hallway. One couple complained that the children playing in the hallway kept them up all night, but there were not children booked into the hotel. This resembles another key scene from *The Shining* with the two young girls in the hallway.

The most haunted rooms are said to be rooms 217, 401, 407, and 418. We tried to find out which room Stephen King stayed in, but there is no public record of which room hosted the

	inspired writer.
	Another ghost of the Stanley hotel is that of Flora Stanley. She entertains guests by playing the piano, but when staff and visitors look inside the room, they see nothing but piano keys moving on their own with no one in sight.
Notes	Paranormal investigators, such as *Ghost Hunters* and *Ghost Adventures* have explored the haunted property on the perimeter of the National Park and boosted its notoriety for being haunted.

Trans-Allegheny Lunatic Asylum

Date	1900s
Location	West Virginia, USA
Type	Haunting
Quantity	Multiple
Evidence	Reports
Description	Trans-Allegheny is yet another lunatic asylum with a powerful paranormal presence which derives from its rich history of injustice, mental illness and death. During its operations from 1864-1994, it mainly served as a psychiatric hospital. In 1913 it was named Weston State Hospital, but changed back to the Trans-Allegheny lunatic asylum more recently when it re-opened as a tourist attraction. You can visit this historic monument in West Virginia and explore the grounds on a ghost tour. The enormous 666 acres consisted of 13 buildings. Read those numbers again. If that's not a good start for a paranormal activity location, who knows what is? Originally built to hold 250 patients in isolation, the asylum saw over 2,400 patients at one time

| | by 1949, including the psychotic Charles Manson.

Over the years it housed mental health patients, victims of epidemics, as well as alcoholics. Thousands of lobotomies were performed on patients there and many out of control patients were put in cages. The doctors there carried out many other inhuman experiments in addition to these.

Those who died there are said to still roam the halls. Ghost hunters and other visitors have reported all the usual paranormal activity you'd expect from a haunted asylum. Apparitions, voices, noises and cold spots that can't be explained.

There have been numerous sightings of the ghost of a civil war soldier as well as patients who resided there until they met their end. There have even been physical attacks on visitors who have been able to show visible marks, caused by the unseen force. |
| Notes | There's even a cemetery on the property which just adds for more hauntings and earns Trans-Allegheny lunatic asylum a place on the top of the list of the most haunted places in America. |

Waverly Hills

Date	1900s
Location	Louisville, Kentucky, USA
Type	Haunting
Quantity	Multiple
Evidence	Reports, Photos, Eye-witnesses
Description	Situated in Kentucky's bustling city of Louisville, the Waverly Hills Sanatorium has become known as one of the most haunted buildings in America and was at one point considered the most haunted place on earth. Tours of the grounds, including sleep-over tours and a Halloween special are offered for those wanting a close-up experience. Waverly Hills opened in 1910 as a tuberculosis hospital during the "White Plague" to house 40 patients back in a time when no cure existed. The hospital expanded over the following years, increasing to a capacity of 400 patients and was considered the most advanced tuberculosis sanatorium in the country. In search of a cure, questionable experiments were conducted, including patients' lungs being exposed to ultraviolet lights in an attempt to stop the spread of the bacteria. Balloons were

surgically inserted into the lungs and then inflated to try and expand the lungs. Ribs and muscles were surgically removed to allow the lungs to expand and accept more oxygen, but most didn't survive the operation. With fresh air also being considered a possible cure, patients were put outside, despite the season. There are even photos of patients covered in snow.

Those who succumbed to illness or experiments had their bodies disposed off through what was called the "body chute". This enclosed tunnel used a motorized system to secretly lower bodies to the railroad at the bottom of the hill so the corpses could be loaded onto trains. This was done so patients wouldn't know how many people were dying as the doctors believed the patients' mental health was as important as their physical health.

Waverly Hills Sanatorium's death toll is exaggerated to claim 50,000-60,000 deaths and some website even claim numbers exceed 145,000, but according to medical records dating back to 1911, the number of deaths was said to be just over 5,000, which is still a hefty number for a single building.

The hospital closed in 1961 due to the development of streptomycin, an anti-biotic that lowered the need for such a hospital.

In 1962, the building was re-opened as Woodhaven Geriatrics Sanitarium to house older residents who received similar mistreatment including electric shock therapy and poor conditions, mainly due to lack of funding, leading the sanatorium to be closed indefinitely in 1982.

Following the shut down of Waverly Hills, it became a place for homeless people looking for shelter, thrill-seekers, explorers and vandals. The building is barely recognizable due to vandalism and the decay over time and it quickly became known as the local haunted house.

Ghost stories started to circulate and the paranormal community began to hear of all the resident ghosts that supposedly lived there. These included the ghost of a little girl who would run up and down the third floor solarium, a man in a white coat in the kitchen, a little boy playing with a leather ball, a woman with bleeding wrists and a phantom hearse that appeared at the back of the sanatorium to drop off coffins.

More reports were of visitors experiencing slamming doors, lights in the windows of a power-less building, strange sounds, cries, screams and footsteps in empty rooms.

The fifth floor has gained much attention with Room 502 being said to have a lot of activity and even unverified claims of people jumping to their deaths from the window.

	More dark events took place in Room 502 including a pregnant nurse hanging herself and another nurse who was stationed in 502 jumping from the roof to her death. With many ghost hunters and explorers capturing pictures and video footage from inside the dark murky sanatorium and the rich history of illness, death and sinister experiments, it's no wonder Waverly Hills has become known as one of the most haunted places on earth.
Notes	The route to Waverly Hills is quite exciting, though that may be the adrenaline of knowing you're about to visit such an iconic place. The Halloween event is really worth your time, but it takes a little of the eeriness out of the experience as it's more of a spectacle.

Yuma Prison

Date	1900s
Location	Arizona, USA
Type	Haunting
Quantity	Multiple
Evidence	Reports, Physical
Description	The Ghosts of the haunted Yuma prison has become a very popular destination for ghost hunters and is considered Arizona's most haunted location. The prison initially opened on July 1, 1876 and operated for 33 years until it shut down on September 15, 1909. Some sources claim that the prison shut down due to overcrowding, and although that's half accurate, the prisoners were actually moved to the newly constructed Arizona State Penitentiary which was located in Florence, Arizona. Yuma prison now stands as a historic museum, but the walls hold something as equally terrifying as the criminals that were housed there over a century ago. The haunted prison has become known as such because of the strange and repetitive reports of

paranormal activity that occurs there and was competing for the most haunted place in America at one point.

The spirits of the prisoner that died on death row are said to wander the historic halls of this desert complex. There have also been many reports of a moaning woman wandering the banks of the Colorado River, said to be looking for her daughter that drowned.

During operations, there were 29 female inmates there, so the ghostly sightings at the haunted prison have a mix of both male and female apparitions.

One ghost that's said to haunt the prison is that of a young girl who will physically interact with visitors, pinching guests before running away. In spite of all this, many people are intrigued by the prison and some even want to experience an overnight stay as it is said that after dark is the most active time for the paranormal occurrences.

Tina Clark, the City of Yuma's Historian and the haunted Yuma prison's doyenne said:

"We have non-profit organizations beg us to let them raffle off an overnight stay here in the prison, but we don't think that's a very good idea."

Notes   ---

Balete Drive

Date	1900s, 2000s
Location	Quezon City, Metro Manila, Philippines
Type	Haunting
Quantity	1+
Evidence	Reports, Eye-Witnesses
Description	Balete Drive in the Philippines has become known for its paranormal phenomena and is considered one of the most haunted places in the country. The street was named Balete Drive after the Balete trees that previously lined the two-lane street, but its real claim to fame is the ghost of the White Lady who is said to haunt it. Referred to by locals as "QC", Quezon City is home to one of the most common ghosts in the world, a White Lady. Though there are many urban legends as to what causes a White Lady (or Lady in White), but the most common seems to be accidental death, murder and suicide. White Lady legends are found in many countries around the world, reportedly seen in rural areas

| | and associated with local legends of tragedy.

The White Lady of Balete Drive has been seen quite frequently and is said to be the ghost of a woman who was raped there (and suggestively died). |
| Notes | We have been there to investigate, but despite numerous reports of a White Lady hitchhiking on the side of the road and even getting in people's vehicles, we were unable to find any traces of her. |

King Montezuma's Treasure

Date	1990s
Location	Three Childs Ranch, Kanab, Utah, USA
Type	Curse
Quantity	1
Evidence	Mysterious deaths, Eye-witnesses
Description	When you think of the greatest lost treasures of the world, King Montezuma and the Aztec cache will be at the top of the list with an estimated value of around $3 billion at today's price, but something overlooked is the unexplained phenomena that may surround it. When Hernan Cortez led the Spanish Conquistadors to the Aztec capital of Tenochtitlan (now Mexico City) in 1519, the Aztecs welcomed them with open arms because their prophecy stated the Aztec God, Quetzalcoatl, would one day return to reclaim his kingdom, and they believed that God to be Cortéz. However, the Spaniard had other plans in mind. The Aztec's showed their false God their gold cache which was a priceless room full of

treasure. Following that, Hernán Cortéz started to execute his plan. The story of what exactly happened after this falls a little bit into the unknown, but the outcome stay the same.

Whether the Spaniards killed most of the Aztecs and King Montezuma in his sleep or if they terrorized the city and murdered Montezuma in the wake of day or whether the citizens of Aztec rebelled and stoned Montezuma to death or if Montezuma was killed in the confusion by the attacks, the fact is, he died in 1519 following the invasion of the Spaniards.

After the Aztec empire had been brought to its knees and King Montezuma was dead, the Spanish headed straight for the treasure room to cash in on their efforts. But Montezuma's trust didn't extend as far as Cortéz thought. The treasure was gone.

Sometime between the Aztecs showing the Spanish their treasure and the death of Montezuma, the Aztecs removed the cache and transported it to a secret location. One that Hernán Cortéz and the conquistadors never found, despite valiant efforts.

Even after alleged torture, the Aztecs either didn't know or refused to disclose where the treasure was moved to and Cortéz reached a dead end, resulting in his dream of getting his hands on the treasure cache ending with failure.

It's said that the Aztecs used a strategy called a water-trap when hiding the treasure, which is a method of tunneling under water to an enclosed area above the water level. They would drain a lake that was situated next to an enclosed cave or cavern. They would then dig a tunnel below the water level far enough beneath the cave and then dig up.

After completing this, they would put the treasure in the cave and then flood the lake again to submerge the tunnel and disguised it completely, then they were said to kill each other on site so their spirits could protect the treasure until the rightful heir came to claim it.

In the present day, the treasure is thought to be just across the Mexican border, in the scenic state of Utah.

Although archaeologists say that the Aztecs considered this their homeland, its a long way for them to carry one of the biggest treasure caches ever recorded. Over 1,800 miles. However, it's entirely possible as there was said to be 8,000 Aztecs moving it. There's also plenty to support the treasure being in Southern Utah. So much so that the Child family purchase the Three Lake Ranch in Kanab, UT.

The family have owned the property for over 30 years and made numerous attempts to access the suspected treasure during that time, but all have failed.

Many theories led to a cave on the property being where the treasure was hidden. Firstly the lake was surrounded by an amber-colored snail which is protected under the Endangered Species Act put in place by the U.S Fish and Wildlife Service.

With draining the lake now off the table, Child hired a professional dive team from California to search the lake for any signs of a tunnel that led towards the cavern.

Each time the divers went into the lake, their equipment malfunction for no reason at all. This happened multiple times until they went down on their final dive and came back with reports of them being suffocated and seeing apparitions in the water.

Now the option option Brandt Child had was to access the cavern from above ground.

He hired a drill company to pierce through the top of the cavern and when the drill piece was removed there was said to be traces of gold on it. This led Child to request a much larger drill, at which point they noticed a figure on a neighboring mountain that they described as an "Aztec warrior staring at them".

However, a larger drill was taken out to the property an drilling began. After the first day, the

	drill operated went home and died of a heart attack and the job could never be completed. The driller's wife died of a heart attack three weeks later and the driller's brother refused to come to the property to pick up the equipment.
Notes	With scuba divers being suffocated, mysterious deaths and a report of an Aztec warrior appearing on the mountain while they were trying to access the treasure, it's no wonder the search was ended. Childs died not long after from a mysterious accident and whether the cavern contains billions of dollars in gold remains a mystery.

Nagoro Village

Date	2000s
Location	Japan
Type	Haunting
Quantity	Multiple
Evidence	Reports
Description	Japan is known as a nation that create bone-chilling horror movies, but this haunted doll village is the real thing... An extremely creepy place with the deceased being replaced by life-size dolls.
	Nagoro or Nagoru, now known as the haunted Nagoro Doll Village is situated on the island of Shikoku in Tokushima Prefecture, Japan and holds a vibe that is creepier that a lot of haunted places on Earth.
	Japan is home to one of the most haunted places in the world, Aokigahara Forest, but the haunted doll village shares the spotlight with its realistic life-sized dolls that have been displayed and positioned to replace previous residents.
	The village acts as a tourist attraction for paranormal investigators and people looking to

experience this eerie place.

Located in a remote mountain area, the village had 300 previous residents, but that dropped by nearly 90% by 2015 due to Japan's population decrease.

The dolls started in the early 2000s when Tsukimi Ayano moved back to the village to look after her sick father, but when he finally passed away, she created a life-sized doll that was placed in a field to look like him.

She didn't stop there though. Since then, Ayano has made more than 400 dolls. Many resembled former residents, while others are just imaginary people.

Others soon followed in her footsteps and started creating dolls. The village school that closed in 2012 became a museum of the dolls with two dolls resembling the last two students that were at the school.

The village is located on Route 439 in the Iya Valley if you're interested in visiting to see the many dolls that are scattered around the village making it similar to the town from the movie *House of Wax*. It's quite a unique place as you can imagine.

Notes	The village is said to be very haunted, likely due to the deaths there and dolls of residents that some say are possessed with the spirits.

Underwater Ghost Town

Date	1900s
Location	Fabbriche di Careggine, Italy
Type	Ghost Town
Quantity	---
Evidence	Photos, Eye-witnesses
Description	The beautiful little village of Fabbriche di Careggine in the Italian mountains conceals an underwater Ghost Town that may be about to appear... Again. First founded in the 13th century by a group of blacksmiths, the Italian village of Fabbriche di Careggine became known for its production of iron and was a thriving little medieval village in the heart of the mountains. Residents were moved to another nearby town, Vagli di Sotto, as construction began on a hydroelectric dam in 1947. The now-abandoned village was flooded in order to create Lake Vagli, but the village's stone structures, bridge, church and foundations managed to remain intact under the water. Since the dam's construction that buried this little village like a deep-sea ship wreck on the ocean

bed, the lake has only been emptied four times between 1947 and 2020 in order to conduct maintenance work. Each time the water was drained, the ghost town would slowly emerge. The last time it surfaced was in 1994.

Thousands of people fled to Fabbriche di Careggine to walk along its streets and view the medieval marvel.

The pictures that were taken from the last appearances show its stone houses, cemetery, bridge and the Church of St Theodore, with its bell tower ruins that leave many in awe.

Though the structures are now submerged under the water, the ghost town is likely to resurface again soon according to the daughter of the ex-mayor of Vagli di Sotto.

	As stated in her Facebook post, Lorenza Giorgio claims that the lake will be emptied in 2021. She wrote: *"I inform you that from certain sources I know that next year, in 2021, Lake Vagli will be emptied."*
Notes	It has been reported since that the energy company which owns the dam (ENEL) has said it's considering draining it as a possibility to boost tourism in the area, however the Covid-19 pandemic may delay the plans.

A History of Vampirism

Date	---
Location	---
Type	Supernatural
Quantity	Multiple
Evidence	---
Description	Though many of the rules of vampirism are made for movies and television, there is one that stands true and that's that only a vampire can make another vampire, which begs the question, how was the first vampire created and where did vampirism originate? Very few would think it, but the origin of vampires has been claimed to date back as far as Ancient Greece with the story of a young man named Ambrogio would was cursed by the Gods, according to the scriptures of Delphi. There's been much confusion over both the authenticity of the scriptures as well as the source. The scripture was written by man with an alleged link through his family's lineage to Ancient Greece. Fandom claim the writings only date back as far as the late 1800s at best, which is accurate based on where they originated.

Others are on the fence about the scriptures, divided between two areas, one being they are complete fantasy and the other being that they are a pillar of ancient mythology. We found where the scriptures claimed to have originated, but will let you make your own mind up whether or not the story is genuine.

Whatever the truth, the man who wrote the scriptures is long gone so there's no way to confirm or deny the legitimacy of the story, as with most mythology. There may be some truth to it and it may well be the true origin of vampires.

The Scriptures of Delphi

According to the scriptures of Delphi, an Italian man named Ambrogio traveled from his home in Italy to Delphi n Greece (no date provided, thought to be around 450BC) to have his prophecy told by the Oracle of Delphi. The oracle was said to be created by Apollo.

Upon arriving in Greece, Ambrogio went straight to the Pythia (oracles) at Apollo's Temple who's words to him were "The curse. The sun. The blood will run."

In one of the days following, Ambrogio met a woman named Selene, who was described in the scriptures as a maiden of Apollo's Temple.

Ambrogio and Selene would rendezvous each

morning at Apollo's Temple and during the young Italian man's time in Greece, they fell in love. With Ambrogio scheduled to leave, he declared his love for Selene by asking her to marry him and return with him to Italy.

The scripts state that Apollo, seeing this, was infuriated that this young man thought he could take a maiden from his temple without even seeking permission, leading Apollo to curse Ambrosio.

Apollo cursed Ambrosio so that if he went out into the sun, his skin would burn, similar to how vampire skin does in modern day movies and books.

Unable to rendezvous with his love outside the temple the next morning, due to the sun curse Apollo had thrust upon him, Ambrogio sought cover in a nearby cave. This was where he met Hades, the God of the Underworld. Hades was the brother of Zeus (Artemis and Apollo's father) and Poseidon, which would make Hades uncle to Artemis and Apollo, who were twins.

Ambrogio explained his predicament to Hades and his love for Selene, upon which, the God of the underworld offered him a deal. Hades told Ambrogio that he would give him a wooden bow with magical properties along with 11 arrows to hunt with. He was told to offer these to Artemis to gain her favor and steal her silver bow. In return, Hades would give him and Selene protection in the underworld so they could be together for eternity.

As collateral, Ambrogio was required to leave his soul with Hades until he returned with the bow, but if he returned without the bow, he would be condemned to the underworld for all eternity, never to see his love again. Ambrosio saw no other option and took the deal.

Having no way to contact Selene to inform her of what had happened, he took his new bow and arrow and killed a swan to use the blood as ink to write her a letter to let her know the situation. He left the letter at their meeting place before sunrise. Selene was said to be devastated, but continued to work at the temple to prevent any more problems from Apollo. The next morning, Ambrosio left her a poem.

This ordeal last for 44 days, each day, Ambrogio slew a swan. He would take the body of the swan to Artemis as a tribute. He was playing two angles. If he could steal the bow, mission accomplished, but if not then he may be able to get Artemis to convince her brother, Apollo, to remove the sun curse.

The scripture states that on the 45th night, Ambrogio used his last arrow, but missed the swan (I assume he reused the arrows as Hades only gave him 11). Artemis noticed he was a fine hunter and a dedicated follower and approached him (Artemis was the Goddess of the hunt and wilderness).

Ambrosio begged her to let him borrow her infamous hunting bow so he could kill one last swan to leave a letter for Selene. Taking pity on him, Artemis agreed and let him borrow the silver bow and arrow. He ran to the cave in a panic to give it to Hades, but Artemis realized she'd been conned by the desperate Ambrogio and put her own curse on him that would make his skin burn if he ever touched silver.

He dropped Artemis' bow and fell to the ground in pain (suggestively before he got to the cave).

Artemis was furious, but Ambrogio begged for her forgiveness, explaining why he did it, the curse her brother had placed on him and his love for Selene. He also shared the deal he'd made with Hades.

Hearing his plea for forgiveness and his terribly unfortunate situation, Artemis took pity and offered him "one last deal".

Artemis offered to make Ambrogio an elite hunter with only her skills being superior to him. She granted him the speed and strength of a God with fangs to "drain the blood of the beasts" to write his poems and letters to Selene.

She also granted him the gift of immortality which means although he had to live with these curses, he could live forever.

In exchange for giving him this new-found power, Artemis wanted he and Selene to escape from Apollo's temple and solely worship her. Though Artemis was a virgin Goddess and her followers had to strictly adhere to the same rules. The two could never be intimate or have children.

Although this was far from ideal, at least they could be together, so he agreed to Artemis' terms. The next morning there was a letter waiting for Selene, prompting her to escape to the boat dock, which she did before Apollo could notice.

Selene fled to the boat dock where she found Ambrosio on his ship. There was a wooden coffin with a note for Selene, telling her to order the captain to set sail and to only open the coffin after sunset. (There's no reasons for Ambrogio being in a coffin when he could have just hidden somewhere on the ship to shield himself from the sun.)

Allegedly the couple sailed to Ephesus, another ancient city in Greece, where they lived in a cave during the day to avoid Ambrogio being exposed to sunlight and they worshipped Artemis in the night at her Grand Temple.

The story states that the couple lived happily together for years whilst abiding by Artemis' rule, but eventually Selene aged while Ambrogio remained immortal and maintained his youth.

On her deathbed, Ambrogio was distraught because his soul remained with Hades and he could not join her in the afterlife, this prompted him to go back to Artemis and beg for Selene to be granted immortality so she could live.

Artemis granted him this favor after their years of loyal worship and told him that he could drink her blood. Doing this would kill her mortal body, but from that day on if their blood was mixed, it would create eternal life for anyone that drank it. Artemis would also see to it that they stayed together forever if he did this.

Ambrogio initially wanted to refuse, but Selene pushed him to agree, so after much convincing, he bit her neck and sucked her blood, just like a modern day vampire would. Ambrosio did what Artemis asked. As her limp body was set down, she began to radiate with light and levitate until she raised up to the skies.

Ambrosio watched on as Selene's spirit raised higher and higher until it met Artemis at the moon and when she arrived, the moon lit up a brilliant white. This was the point when Selene became the Goddess of the Moon.

"Every night she [Selene] would reach down with her rays of light to the earth and finally touch her beloved Ambrogio as well as all of their children – the newly created vampires who carried the

blood of Ambrogio and Selene, together."

Ambrogio was said to eventually return to Italy, but the story of what happened to him after that is unknown. Some say he created a clan of vampires that ended in civil war. Others say he is still alive today, residing somewhere in Florence.

One of the discrepancies we found in the scripts of Delphi to confirm it was in fact the origin of vampires is that Selene was well known to have an affair with a mortal named Endymoin who she was said to have fifty children with, though this could have been an affair and the children that were referred to weren't Ambrosio's.

It was said that Selene was also one of Zeus' lovers and the two had many children; Pandia, she who is all-bright; Ersa, the dew; Nemea, the nymph of the eponymous place; and Dionysus, although this may be a confusion due to the name similarity between Selene and Semele.

There are also sources stating that Selene, who wasn't a virgin Goddess like Artemis, had children with Tithonus, a Trojan Prince. Selene was also mentioned to date a god named Pan, but throughout history, there hasn't been any mentioned of an "Ambrogio". Furthermore, many believe that Selene was actually an older Goddess than Artemis, who in some ways replaced her.

<u>Tuberculosis, The Consumption and the New</u>

<u>**England Vampire Panic -1888**</u>

When European settlers first came to North America, they considered the vast forests a place of unease where supernatural entities were hidden as well as a place for witches and demons to conduct their dark rituals and magic. Europeans brought many beliefs and myths with them that paired well with supernatural myths and dark forests, including the belief that corpses would return from the dead and feed on the living.

These creatures went by many names in European Folklore: the revenant, the aptganger, and of course the most well-known; the vampire.

Later in the late 1800s, New England announced a "Vampire Panic" due to many people turning pale and dying. The true cause was a tuberculosis outbreak, better known as "The White Plague" but that didn't stop bodies being exhumed, examined and even having organs burned to prevent the dead from returning to drain the life-force from the living.

This event lasted many years and despite the true cause of the "vampire panic" being tuberculosis, many still consider it a basis for vampire belief in modern day.

<u>**Bram Stoker, Count Dracula and Vlad the**</u>

<u>**Impaler – 1897**</u>

Another main source for people's exposure to vampires was Bram Stoker's 1897 novel, Dracula. Although the iconic story was not published until the end of the 19th century, the inspiration for the character was said to come from a much earlier time.

In 1456, Vlad the Impaler or Vlad III Draculea) Vlad Dracula) was credited with killing many people by ways of impalement, which ultimately earned him the name Vlad the Impaler.

In 1490, a monk who referred to Vlad III as a fierce, but just ruler, wrote the book "The Tale of Dracula" which shared many of the legends of Vlad. Nearly 400 years later, Bram Stoker released Dracula, which was inspired by Vlad.

Despite Vlad being the inspiration for Stoker's epic character, history suggests that other than the name, "Dracula", and a taste for blood, the real-life Dracula and the fictional character shared nothing in common.

Also, Bran Castle in Transylvania, which was considered Dracula's castle, had no link to Vlad III whatsoever. There is no evidence that he even stepped foot in the castle.

Notes	Everything from The New England Vampire, Interview with the Vampire, Twilight, The Vampire Diaries and Blade have taken some

kind of inspiration from these to shape the world
and rules of vampires as we know.

Epping Forest

Date	Multiple
Location	Essex, England
Type	Haunting
Quantity	Multiple
Evidence	Eye-witnesses, Reports
Description	Epping Forest is an area of ancient woodland in England. It's a former royal forest and is managed by the City of London corporation. The size and density of Epping Forest have made it a popular hideout for criminals and an infamous burial spot for bodies. Notorious highwayman Dick Turpin hid there in the early 1700s and more than a dozen murder victims have been discovered in the woods since the 1960s.
	The forest is thought to have been given legal status as a royal forest by Henry II in the 12th century. This status allowed commoners to use the forest to gather wood and foodstuffs, and to graze livestock and turn out pigs for mast, but only the king was allowed to hunt there.
	It's no surprise then that the forest has developed a reputation for spooky sounds and ghostly apparitions. Some people also claim that if you drive to Hangman's Hill and park in neutral, your car will slowly be pulled uphill.

A number of accounts have reported muffled sounds of drums and marching emanating from the forest, and some people believe that this is caused by the spirits of dead soldiers. Several reports have been made over the years of spirits apparently taking material form.

In the 1960s, there were sightings of ghostly figures emerging from a pond near Lindsey Street in Epping. The figures were said to emerge from the pond on horseback before riding towards town and disappearing. Another pond at an unknown location deep in the woods is said to draw people to commit suicide in its murky waters, after two young lovers died in a tragic murder-suicide at the pond many centuries ago.

Even if you don't believe in the myths, just the appearance of the woods is likely to send a chill up your spine. The pollarded trees haven't been cut since the late 1800s giving them an overgrown and bulbous look that you won't find anywhere else. Restless spirits have also been blamed for Epping Forest's most well-known and bizarre supernatural phenomenon that persists to this day.

| Notes | --- |

Inspiration for A Nightmare on Elm Street

Date	1970s
Location	Cambodia
Type	Haunting, Mysterious
Quantity	Multiple
Evidence	Reports
Description	Wes Craven's 1984 masterpiece, *A Nightmare on Elm Street*, was certainly original, as was Freddy Krueger, who almost instantly became the most iconic horror legend of all time. Though the dream-stalking child murderer with severely burned skin was created from Wes' imagination, many people may not know that the concept was actually inspired by a true story that that's paranormal activity is overlooked. The inspiration for A Nightmare on Elm Street came from a family Craven read about in the L.A Times during the 1970s that survived the killing fields of Cambodia and fled to the United States. The family escaped, but the youngest son suffered terrible dreams and couldn't shake the thoughts of someone chasing and tormenting him while he slept. The nightmares became worse, even to the point he was scared to sleep

and stayed awake for days. Craven stated:

"He told his parents he was afraid that if he slept, the thing chasing him would get him, so he tried to stay awake for days at a time. When he finally fell asleep, his parents thought this crisis was over. Then they heard screams in the middle of the night. By the time they got to him, he was dead. He died in the middle of a nightmare. Here was a youngster having a vision of a horror that everyone older was denying. That became the central line of Nightmare on Elm Street."

The cause for death was mysterious and unexplained, but in 1981, the CDC started monitoring more mysterious nocturnal deaths which occurred in male immigrants from Laos, Vietnam and Cambodia and there seemed to be some kind of a connection.

"In 1981, the peak year of these deaths, 26 men, often Hmong refugees from the highlands of northern Laos, died in their sleep. Usually victims were simply found dead, but when medics arrived quickly, the men's hearts were fibrillating or contracting wildly, a symptom Parrish said may result from numerous possible causes." -LA Times

The term is actually known as 'SUNDS' which stands for 'Sudden Unexplained Nocturnal Death Syndrome'. The mysterious disorder was first mentioned in 1917 and originated in the Philippines, a country that's made numerous appearances throughout this almanac.

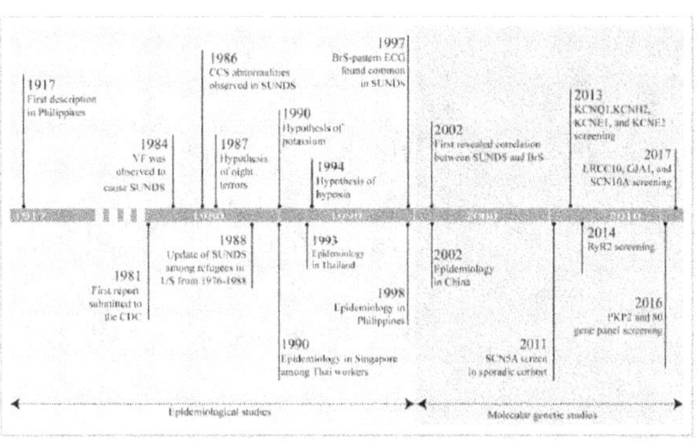

SUNDS didn't attract worldwide attention until 1981 when the first report was submitted to the Centers for Disease Control and Prevention (CDC), which just so happens to be the same year Wes Craven finished the first script for *A Nightmare on Elm Street.*

Medical experts attributed the young boy's death to the same reason, but SUNDS isn't specifically linked to dreams. Another reason the boy died in his dream could have been a heart attack. It's very rare to have a dream that scares you to the point of heart attack, especially for a younger person, but it is possible and with the boy's psychological state after enduring such a brutal experience in the killing fields of Cambodia, it may have been the cause.

Whatever the reason, Craven took the story which fueled the inspiration for Freddy and he developed the first script for A Nightmare on Elm Street. The movie was released in 1984 and

	didn't take long to light up the horror world with the Springwood Slasher terrifying fans who got to see it on the big screen.
Notes	Directly linked to the Cambodian killing fields was the Tuol Sleng where thousands of people were imprisoned and tortured in the most inexplicable way. The Tuol Sleng Genocide Museum is considered extremely haunted.

The Ancient Ram Inn

Date	Multiple
Location	Wotton-UnderEdge, England
Type	Satanic Worship, Witchcraft, Haunting, Poltergeist
Quantity	Multiple
Evidence	Reports, Physical, Eye-witness, Worship items, Skeletal remains, Ley Lines
Description	With nearly 900 years of supernatural history, the Ancient Ram Inn has become of the most haunted places in the world. It's located at 8 Potters Pond in Wotton-under-Edge, about 100 miles west of London.
	As with many other haunted places in England, this building has an incredible history.
	The Ancient Ram Inn was originally built in 1145, directly on top of an ancient pagan burial ground. If that's not reason enough to make it haunted, the building also sits directly over the intersection of two Ley Lines which are said to be a point of high spiritual energy.
	Similar to the Hellfire Caverns that may draw energy from the Ley Lines, many say that Stonehenge feeds spiritual energy to the Inn

which provides the fuel the dark entities feed on.

Following all that, it served as a priest's house and then a brewery, but in 1968 it poured its last pint. It was purchased by the late John Humphries shortly after and acted as a bed & breakfast while he fought to save the building until his death in 2017.

Unlike the majority of haunted places in England and other countries, the ghosts of the Ancient Ram Inn are far more sinister and malicious than your typical spooky shadow.

There are many ghosts that people claim to have identified and traced at the Ancient Ram Inn, most of which are bone-chilling.

The owner himself reported that on his first night staying there he was dragged out his bed and across the room by an unseen force.

One of the best known ghosts of the Ancient Ram Inn is a witch who was burned at the stake in the 1500s. She took refuge in the house before she was captured and killed. The room where she is most frequently spotted is now called "The Witch's Room", said to be haunted by her ghost.

Another room in the building, which is said to be haunted by a monk, was given the name "The Bishop's Room". Guests who stayed at the Inn declined the offer to stay in the Bishop's room after other guests who'd stayed in there were terrified enough to flee the property in the middle of the night, literally screaming as they scarpered up the street.

Another came from a plumber who was doing work at the Inn. He reported a centurion on horseback that passed straight through a solid wall in front of him. Others have claimed that a succubus creeps into visitor's beds while they sleep.

Humphries kept the Ancient Ram Inn as a haunted bed & breakfast, but did make some very eerie discoveries.

Humphries found evidence of devil worship and ritual sacrifice hidden on the grounds. He also found the skeletal remains of children under the stairs, some with broken daggers that had been thrust into their chests.

Since John Humphries' death in 2017, it was taken over by his wife, Caroline Humphries. In 2019, she shared her future plans for the building with The Wotton Times and invited archaeologists to investigate there.

The Ancient Ram Inn has built up such a reputation, a large majority of the locals won't even walk past the property after dark and the Inn is considered one of Britain's most haunted places.

Notes	---

The Tower of London

Date	Multiple
Location	London, England
Type	Haunting
Quantity	Multiple
Evidence	Reports
Description	The Tower of London has a long rich British history from being the home of kings and queens to the brutal events, collectively making it known as one of the most haunted places in England.
	Built in 1078 by William the Conqueror, the Tower served as a prison among other things for the majority of its existence until 1952, incluing being the residence of the Royal Family.
	Visitors have reported ghost sightings for many years including apparitions, shadow anomalies and even clear faces in photos when no one else was present in the picture.
	Some of most frequent sightings include the ghost of Queen Anne Boleyn, who was beheaded at the Tower on May 19, 1536, under the orders of her husband, Henry VIII, just after she had a still birth.

Many people have reported seeing her headless body walking the corridors as well as her being spotted near her execution site. She's also been seen leading a procession down the aisle of a chapel.

Other reports from people claiming to see the ghost of Anne Boleyn include her walking with her own severed head under her arm.

More recently, two skeletal remains were found in the tower. Discovered in 1938, the skeletons are believed by historians to be the the remains of Edward V and his brother Richard of Shrewbury, Duke of York.

Aged 9 and 12 years old, they were locked in the tower by their uncle, Richard III. Though it's not confirmed, a common hypothesis is that they were murdered by their uncle in an attempt for him to secure his throne.

Their deaths likely occurred in 1483, but their remains were discovered in the 20th century and the stories of their ghosts haunting the tower, as well as many other spirits, are still prevalent.

Notes	---

The Villisca House

Date	June 9, 1912
Location	Villisca, Iowa, USA
Type	Haunting
Quantity	Multiple
Evidence	Reports, Eye-witnesses
Description	On June 9, 1912, Josiah Moore, his wife, two children and two of his children's friends were mysterious murdered in their sleep by an ax-wielding killer. Or killers. The ax was left against the wall in the house, but the case is unsolved. One prime suspect, a traveling preacher, George Kelley, confessed to the crime in 1918, but later withdrew his confession and the trial resulted in a hung jury. The person in charge of running the ghost tours, Johnny Houser, claims to have seen doors swing open, object move, chairs rock and voices, but has never seen a ghost himself. Other skeptics who have stayed at the property have reported all of the above and much more.
Notes	You can book a night at the Villisca House.

The Whaley House

Date	1800s, 1990s
Location	San Diego, California, USA
Type	Haunting
Quantity	Multiple
Evidence	Reports, Eye-witness, Smells, Physical
Description	Labelled at one point as the most haunted house in America by LIFE Magazine, the Whaley House was built over a graveyard and it served as a courthouse in the 1800s were many criminals were hung. Built in 1853, just after Thomas Whaley's move to the west in 1849 during the gold rush, he claimed it was the best house in San Diego. Thomas and his wife, Anna, lived there with their six children. Thomas died in downtown San Diego from natural causes in 1890. His wife passed away in the house in 1913. Researchers claim you can sometimes smell Thomas' cigar smoke and Anna's lavender perfume in the house. The most visible and active ghost is said to be that of Yankie Jim Robinson, allegedly present

	before the house was built. He was executed at the gallows on the property for stealing a rowboat, before the Whaley House was built. It's thought that he was innocent and that's why his ghost haunts the Whaley House. His spirit is often seen in the master bedroom. Another ghost that has been frequently reports is Violet Whaley, At age 22, she went to the outhouse one morning and took her own life after a bad marriage. She shot herself in the chest, but not before she left a note on the porch that read: *"Mad from life's history, swift to death's mystery, glad to be hurled, anywhere, anywhere out of this world."* She was alive when they found her and was brought inside before passing away in the guest bedroom.
Notes	Dana White, the president of the UFC, even requested that he get marked while on a ghost tour in the house. He went to the doorway where a spirit was hung and said he was not a believer. He wasn't convinced and received no mark. (you can see the episode on Youtube; Looking for a Fight San Diego).